GOD IS IN THE DARKNESS:

FINDING FAITH IN TROUBLED TIMES

CLARKE K. OLER

GOD IS IN THE DARKNESS

Finding Faith In Troubled Times

CLARKE K. OLER

A Bartleby Book
Published by Bartleby Books

Printed in The United States of America

7 6 5 4 3 2 1

First printing: September 2006
Revision 2-100906

Publisher Cataloging-in-Publication Data
Oler, Clarke K.
God Is In the Darkness / Clarke K. Oler
          p.   cm.
ISBN 10: 0-9787651-0-9
ISBN 13: 978-0-9787651-0-1
1. Clarke K. Oler. 2. Religion—United States—Autobiography 3. Psychology, Religious
I. Title

Distributed by Lightning Source, Inc., 1246 Heil Quaker Blvd., La Vergne, TN, USA, 37086
(615) 213-5815, Fax: (615) 213-4426

Cover and book design by Jef Clarke

To Wendy,
my cherished life companion,

loyal friend, splendid mother,
funny and feisty and irrepressibly generous,

who never missed a sermon or talk,
and filled me up with her love
and unquenchable appetite for life.

ACKNOWLEDGMENTS

I want to thank the circle of close friends who met with me over the course of a summer to read and assess this collection: Bob Shull, who spent uncountable hours transcribing them and preparing the notes, Marianne Ryan, Steve Galton, Bill Doulos, Win Griffen, Harry Evans, Mark Rice, and Amy Phillips.

I also would like to thank Margaret Marsh, who did a generous amount of proofreading, Jef Clarke, my publishing consultant, and William Sloane Coffin, life-long friend and North Star on my path to the ministry, John Burt, George Regas and Ed Bacon, successive rectors of All Saints Church, Pasadena, who exemplified the heartfulness and courage of our vocation.

And thank you to all those in the congregations who were inspired by these sermons and talks, and encouraged me to preserve them.

꧁

"This is the ground of religion. It rests upon a trust and a faith that for the religious man have become his deepest certainty, the certainty of faith, not the certainty of logic. The certainties of logic leave our wills untouched...I am persuaded that God is greater than logic, although not contrary to logic, and our mere inability to catch Him in the little net of our human reason is no proof of His non-existence, but only of our need that our little reason shall be supplemented by His tender visitations, and that He may lead and guide us to the end of the road in ways superior to any that our intellects can plan. This is the blindness of trust, which walks with Him, unafraid, into the dark."

—Thomas R. Kelly
The Reality of the Spiritual World

꧁

CONTENTS

PREFACE

No one is an expert in the Christian life. Most of us make our way through life trying to follow the example of Jesus the best way we know how. But sometimes our burdens seem insupportable and our fears are overwhelming. We come to church reaching out to a God who will help us through the darkness. I believe that we all come to God seeking understanding and hope. And I believe that God meets us where we are, to give us the courage to endure and to grow.

The sermons and talks in this collection were all given at All Saints Episcopal Church, Pasadena, California, except "The Boy and the Crèche." They are expressions of my own faith forged over fifty years as a parish priest. Sometimes my own fears and shame have seemed to block out any sense of God's presence, as dark clouds block out the sun's light. So I am no stranger to the cries and whispers of my flock. Whenever I have sat down to write a sermon or talk, I have tried to listen first to my own heart for the questions and cares that others might bring to their worship of God. Then I share the faith that that I have received over the years as God has pursued me like the "hound of heaven," in sorrow and joy, in my emptiness, and in my sense of hope and peace that pass human understanding.

There is an old saying that God comforts the afflicted, and afflicts the comfortable. It takes courage to open ourselves to God and risk finding nothing, or feeling judged. The word "courage" comes from the French: "an act of the heart." Faith is an act. We seize God's promise of life and apply it as a balm to our aching hearts. It is not a simple thing to trust Him. But I believe He alone possesses the secret of our common humanity and the peace which we seek in the deep places of our spirit.

Roger Schutz, the late Prior of the Community of Taizé, wrote: "In every person lies a zone of solitude that no human intimacy can fill. There God encounters us. There in the depth is set the intimate festival of the risen Christ... So henceforth in the hollow of our being we discover the risen Christ, and He is our festival."

I hope those who read these sermons and talks will be helped to find their own path to that blessed encounter, and will, in their own time, experience the inexplicable mercy of God's love.

I often refer to God as "He" because it is the habit of a lifetime. I know that God possesses all that is feminine and masculine. Through a connection that is fully resonant and deeply personal, we each identify with God in our own way.

—*Clarke K. Oler*

1

THE BOY AND THE CRÈCHE

The snow was already falling, huge flakes spiraling down, covering the lawn in front of The Church of the Holy Trinity. Christmas Eve service would not begin for three hours, and I stood at the window of the second floor sitting room in the Rectory, calculating how deep the snow would get. The sexton and I would have to shovel the path and steps for the arriving worshippers.

Eighty-Eighth Street was dark and empty. The usual pedestrians must have been already at home with their families. There were only two streetlights trying to illuminate the sidewalk in front of the church. I had been meaning to speak to the city department in charge of streetlights about that. It never seemed bright enough.

But at Christmas time that was a slight advantage, because every year we erected a large crèche in the church garden with nearly life-sized figures in a plywood shed that was lighted on the inside. In the dim light of the street our crèche was easily visible.

There were the usual figures of the Holy Family: Joseph standing beside the seated figure of Mary, who gazed lovingly at the baby Jesus in the wooden crib. A shepherd held a plaster lamb in his arms, and three elegant Kings bearing gifts knelt before the manger. A thick carpet of straw covered the ground at their feet. The straw was a gift from the mounted police in Central Park, who delivered several bales faithfully every year. The crèche was a well-known feature in the neighborhood for many years at Christmas time.

Then I saw him, the little boy about six years old. He was peering through the fence at the crèche. I recognized the red wool hat pulled down over his ears, the frayed jacket and tattered jeans. I had seen him on the street often and had tried to get to know him; but, every time I had approached him, he had stared at me for a moment with solemn eyes and then had turned and run away. Now he was back, staring at the crèche.

The snow covered everything. The tops of the huge square brick gateposts sported white Tam o' Shanters of snow. And it lay like a winter blanket on the roof of the plywood shed. But the inside of the crèche looked warm and inviting.

As I watched, the little boy walked quickly into the garden, across the snow to the crèche, and climbed inside. In less than a moment, he was lying on his back in the straw, looking up at the face of the Holy Mother. I saw his hand reach up and touch her cheek.

Fifteen minutes went by. I could just see the top of his red cap and his hand reaching up now and then to touch the kind face of the Virgin. Then all of a sudden something startled him. In an instant he was up and running across the snow and out the gate.

I never saw him again. In the years that have followed, on Christmas Eve I think of him, of my inability to engage him, of the tender moments in the crèche. I have wondered what has become of him, and whether it is possible that some gift of comfort and hope was given him in those few minutes when he lay in the straw and reached up to touch the face of God.

2

GOD IS IN THE DARKNESS

Advent is the beginning of the Church year, a kind of prologue to the Christian story. It is a season of four weeks beginning on the last Sunday in November in which we recall the centuries during which Israel struggled to understand and come to terms with God. The birth of Jesus is God's answer to their dilemma and despair.

At another level, Advent is a season in which we reflect upon our own struggle with our own faith, our failure and guilt at losing touch with God, especially when we need Him most in times of our greatest pain.

It is not a bright, cheerful season. There is a dark, brooding quality to it. The altar colors have turned to deep purple. We have been lighting the Advent candles slowly, one week at a time. The Christ candle is still unlit, withholding its promised light until the fullness of time on

Christmas Eve. The music of our Advent services—often written in minor keys—has a somber, contemplative quality.

The most well known Advent hymn is "O Come, O Come Emmanuel." Listen to some of its words:

> O Come, O Come Emmanuel,
> And ransom captive Israel,
> That mourns in lonely exile here…
> Disperse the gloomy clouds of night...
> Bid thou our sad divisions cease...

"Captive," "lonely exile," "gloomy clouds of night," "sad divisions": these words express the dark and painful experience of Israel in its battle to get it right with God. These words also reflect our experience in our own sometimes losing battle for a faith that works for us in the hardest of times.

It is hard for the Church to maintain the somber mood of its Advent services because the tradesmen have stolen Advent. Thanksgiving is barely over when the stores and television are blaring Christmas carols and bedecking themselves in Christmas decorations. It didn't use to be so in earlier times. In the old days, Advent was truly a season of self-examination and penitence. And Christmas parties were not held until *after* Christmas, in the season we call Twelfth Night. When I was a young and foolish priest in my first parish, I tried to salvage Advent by asking my congregation to hold off on Christmas parties until after Christmas. I almost got run out of my parish by outraged parishioners who couldn't believe I would even think of such a thing.

The central message of Advent is that God is not just a light at the end of a dark tunnel. God is in the dark tunnel with us. In the dark times of our lives we struggle to be faithful to God in spite of doubt and failure and guilt. And we struggle with the pain of grief and fear and illness and personal calamities. It is crucial for us to hold on to the belief that God is with us in those hard times. He doesn't just suddenly show up when things get better.

The Bible often implies that God is only in the light; that the darkness is ruled by Satan. That is not true. Remember, in the first chapter of Genesis it says that in the act of Creation, God separated the light from the dark; he created the day and the night, and he said that it is *good!* The day is the time for work and caring for our families. The night is the time for rest and renewal. It is as though God turns the lights out so we can go to sleep; he doesn't go away when the lights go out. He is like our parents when we were little children and were afraid of the dark, and they said to us, "Don't be afraid. We are just in the next room. Call us if you have a bad dream."

One of my favorite psalms is Psalm 139, in which the Psalmist cries out to God in grateful wonder:

> Where shall I go from thy spirit? Or where
> shall I go from thy presence?
> If I climb up to heaven, thou art there; if I
> go down to hell, thou art there also.
> Though I say, perhaps the darkness will
> engulf me, yet shall my night be turned into
> day.
> For the darkness is no darkness with thee,
> but the night is as clear as the day; the
> darkness and the light to thee are both alike.

I have a friend who from the time she was a little girl wanted to be a nun. When she graduated from high school, she joined a religious order. For twenty years she was a conscientious and devoted nun. But during those twenty years she experienced a growing apprehension that she did not really belong in the religious life—that she had made a too-hasty choice as a young woman. But she stuck it out, trying her best to make it work. Still, her joy in serving God was suffused with the growing shadow of doubt about her vocation. Finally she found the courage to make the decision to leave the order. It was the darkest day of her life. She was terrified because she knew little of life in the outside world and she was leaving her closest friends; but she knew in her heart of hearts that it was right.

She told me what it was like on that fateful day when she walked out of the convent with practically no money, no job, and no place to go. She rented a room at the YWCA, went into her tiny room, closed the door and leaned back against it. As the fear rose up in her, she looked at the ceiling and said out loud, "Okay, God. What do I do now?" Well, God did lead her to a job in a gift shop, and he led her to a happy marriage. The years in the convent were dark years as she waited and prayed and formed her decision. But it never occurred to her that God was not in that darkness with her, guiding, comforting, and encouraging her. Yes, God was in the light at the end of the tunnel, but he was with her in the darkness, too.

The movie *Shadowlands* tells the story of C. S. Lewis' all-too-brief marriage to Joy. He was in his mid-sixties; she was many years younger and was dying of bone cancer when they were married. He said in his autobiography that he couldn't believe that he could find in his later years the joy that had eluded him all his life. They feasted on love!

But Lewis was so overwhelmed by her suffering and the prospect of her death that he could not bring himself to talk to her about it. Finally, Joy took him by the hand and gently but urgently pleaded with him to talk with her about her dying. If he doesn't, she told him, the loneliness of her dying would be unbearable; that if God is in the victory *after* death, then God must also be in the dying! She says, "The pain now is part of the joy later. That's the deal!"

So Lewis is drawn into the shadowland of her dying. As they share their sorrow and pain with each other, they are drawn closer together and their love becomes even richer and deeper. They also share their hope and their laughter. In his journal he records, "Once very near the end I said to Joy, 'If you can—if it is allowed—come to me when I too am on my death bed.' 'Allowed!' she cried. 'Heaven would have a job to hold me, and as for Hell, I'd break it into bits.' There was a twinkle in her eye as well as a tear." They found an intense and buoyant love that they did not believe possible. Lewis had written many books about theology and pain and God's love, but he had never experienced them in so deeply personal a way. In those precious days he came to understand that such tender intimacy, that incredible bond—that love they shared— was God's Holy Spirit in their life in the land of shadows.

What might be your unique advents, your shadowlands that you bring to this Advent season?

- Maybe you have lost someone dear to you; you come home night after night to an empty house;

the loneliness in unbearable. That is *your* shadowland. A man whose wife of fifty years had died a short time before said to me, "My bed is so empty! I just put my arms around the pillow as though it were she, and cry myself to sleep."

· Maybe you feel your faith slipping away; you sit in church, numb. It doesn't move you the way it used to. Your prayers turn to dust in your mouth. That is *your* shadowland.

· I know what that feels like. I know the emptiness of sitting down to write a sermon and feeling as though I have nothing more to say to my flock, nothing fresh, nothing helpful, wondering if I should still be a priest. It was my own shadowland.

· Maybe you said something hurtful to someone, you can't take it back; you should bite your tongue off. Someone is suffering needlessly because of you. You feel ashamed. That is *your* shadowland.

· Maybe you are trying to cope with an illness, you can't seem to get your strength back; you are depressed and afraid. That is *your* shadowland.

I can remember lying in a hospital bed. The doctor had just told my wife that there was nothing he could do for me, that we should go home and get our affairs in order. I stared at the ceiling; the prayers wouldn't come. What was I, a priest, doing here, unable to call upon my own faith when I needed it most? I remember hearing what seemed like a voice say to me, "It's going to be all right." I knew instinctively that God was speaking to me, that it did not mean I was going to get well, only that it didn't matter. If I got well it would be all right; if I died it would be all right. Either way I would be with him. God was in the darkness and he would be my light.

> O come, thou Dayspring, come and cheer
> Our spirits by thine advent here.
> Let love stir in the womb of night,
> And death's dark shadow put to flight...

We all have our shadowlands, our depressions, our doubts, our illnesses, our griefs. We must learn to open our eyes to see that God is there, not just as some hoped-for cure and solution to our problems. He is in the love, the courage, the creative spirit we bring to each moment in the battle of life.

There is a beautiful moment toward the end of the film *Shadowlands*. After she died, Lewis and Joy's twelve-year-old son are in the attic of the house going through her things. Despite his brilliance as a theologian, he is nearly paralyzed by grief. It seems to him that God has shut him out. Joy's son turns to him, and with all the bravery at his command he says, "I know that Mummy is with God, and I am glad for her... but oh how I miss her!" Lewis puts his arm around him, tears running down his cheeks, and says, "Oh, so do I!" In that moment of sharing their helplessness, the sixty-five-year-old man and the twelve-year-old boy come together at the deepest level of their hearts. God was there.

It has not been my experience that God breaks into this earthly life to protect the innocent. God did not protect the victims of the Holocaust, or the Muslim women of

Kosovo who were snatched from their homes and raped, or the countless innocent men, women and children who have died in automobile accidents. That is not the kind of God that I know, though I have often wished it were. The God I know comes in the darkness to find us, to turn on the light in our hearts, to inspire courage, to give us the will to fight on, to tell the truth in a world full of lies, to choose life in the face of defeat, to improvise love in the face of indifference.

On my bookshelf I have a book that is precious to me. It contains portions of letters from hundreds of men who died in the concentration camps. Letter after letter is a testament to faith that would not die, faith which was the only thing that made their dying bearable, faith that was their last and most precious gift to their wives and children and friends.

One letter was written by Col. Alexis von Renne, a German officer who was executed for his part in the attempt to assassinate Hitler. He wrote, "As my last wish, I entreat you only to cling to the Lord and to have full confidence in Him.... If only you knew with what inconceivable loyalty He is standing by my side at this moment, you would be armoured and calm for all your difficult life. He will give you strength for everything."

I could understand it if some of you might say, "That is not a good enough deal. I want a safer world, and I want a God who can give it to me. If not, I choose not to believe in him. I'll make it on my own." But this is the only world there is. It will never be safe from accidents and catastrophes. Greed and brutality and corruption will always be around us in men and women who have shut up their consciences from God. It is up to us to make the world as safe and hopeful as we can by fighting against those evils. The meaning of life is in the fight itself. God is in the struggle for every shred of justice and decency and beauty and peace; he will not let one act of love be wasted. As Joy said, "The pain now is part of the joy later. That's the deal."

God is in the darkness. We cannot wait for the light to come on at Christmas before we choose life. But we know the light is coming. Christ will come, not as a magician to solve our problems, but as a man of sorrows, acquainted with grief, bearing in his flesh the scars from the whips and the nail holes in his hands and feet. He will take us by the hand and walk with us through our shadowlands into such a bright dawn as we cannot yet even imagine.

3

THE HEALING PATH

During a healing service, anyone who wants to may come forward to the altar rail and receive the laying on of hands. We will observe the Church's ancient sacrament of healing and invite you to participate. We hope you will. But we recognize that the laying on of hands, and the Eucharist—which is the greatest of the healing sacraments—have often left our people feeling untouched by God's power to heal. I want to address that question this morning.

The Anglican Church speaks softly about healing because we do not believe in making a spectacle of such things. There is a reticence in our worship and a profound respect for the privacy of each person's spiritual journey.

My sister was a beautiful, dark-eyed girl of nine when she died of pneumonia. She was the only daughter with three brothers in our family, and her death devastated my parents. I was the youngest, just a toddler at the time, too young to understand about her death,; but I was old enough to know that I was her joy, because she had held me and taught me to walk. I wondered where she had gone.

My parents were faithful at church and prayed fervently for her recovery, but that was not to be.

Why would I begin a talk about the healing power of God with a story of my sister's death? Because, in spite of their devastation and the senselessness of her death, there was healing for my parents. A few days after her funeral, my mother was going through Sister's things on her bedside table. There was the little New Testament that Sister had received from her Sunday School class, and which she had loved to read, especially in those final few weeks of her illness. My mother picked it up and it fell open to the place where Sister had placed the ribbon and marked a passage with a pencil. My mother read, "If you love me you will not grieve, because I go to my Father who is in heaven." Those words from St. John settled upon Mother's broken heart as a benediction. The message was clear: all was well with Sister. She had known that it would be so before she died, and she wanted our mother and father to know it too.

Did the prayers for healing fail? In one sense, they surely did. That beautiful young life was not saved. But if receiving assurance of a happy new life for their daughter was a kind of healing for my parents, then whether that assurance came from God, or from Sister, or from some deep well of faith within my parents, or from a combination of all these sources, then it was a healing. Surely God was there beginning to heal their grief in that moment, even though it was not the healing of her body for which they had so urgently prayed.

The healing of grief takes a long time. The sense of loss never completely goes away, nor should it. The depth of grief is the measure of love. But the wracking pain does end. For my parents it began to heal when they read the passage from St. John. The terrible sense of betrayal by God that they must have felt when Sister died began to mend in that moment.

Over the years, I have pursued the healing ministry of the church by laying hands on the sick and troubled. Following the services, we offer that ministry every Sunday for those who choose to come to the altar rail in the chapel. Twice a year we have large healing services in which everyone in the church is invited to come to the rail for the laying on of hands. The same ministry is offered every week at mid-week services. I say I have "pursued" this ministry because I have to admit I have never entirely grasped the ministry of healing; that is, I have never fully understood how it works or even, in some cases, *whether* it works. I never saw anyone throw a crutch away or leave his wheelchair, and sometimes people worsened and died.

But I have pursued this ministry doggedly, faithfully, hopefully, and joyfully. I have laid hands on thousands of people for no other reason than that I believe that God wants them to be whole; that God is the source of all healing. That if we turn to God with trusting hearts, healing will be given though it may not be the kind of healing we are asking for, though we may not see the healing at the time, or know how it is being given. So with utmost sincerity I have wanted to enact, to symbolize, to sacramentalize the connection between our God who desires our wholeness and ourselves who reach out to God in our need.

Some people on whom I have laid my hands have returned to tell me of the deep peace of God they received at that moment, and that in some way they didn't fully understand it was a bridge, an opening to a new life. Not because of me personally; I am just one of God's plumbers hooking up the pipes so that the Holy Spirit of God can flow through to the one who needs it.

I believe that almost all of us, even the most skeptical of us, turn to God when we are in need, when our own resources fail. I remember a buddy of mine in the Army who used to regale me with stories about how he hated the church and all religion because the nuns had bullied him when he was growing up in a Catholic orphanage. It was in World War II, and we were in a battle for a few miles of jungle in the Burma campaign. I had taken cover in a shell hole from a Japanese artillery barrage. Suddenly a shell burst in the trees above me showering shell fragments all around me. My buddy came diving into the hole next to me yelling, "Holy Mary, Mother of God!" I said, "Hey, I thought you didn't believe in God." He replied, "Oh, yeah. I forgot." We laughed, but neither of us was quite as profane after that.

Even when our faith is frail, we reach out from wherever we are on our journey of faith to "thank whatever gods may be" for help we cannot find within ourselves. And when we do, I believe God meets us. Somewhere in the hollow of our being God meets us and claims us. Jesus did that for the thief on the cross beside him, a poor, erring, rough-hewn man who scarcely knew who Jesus was. But in his helplessness and pain he cried out, "Lord, remember me when you come into your kingdom!" Without an instant's hesitation Jesus claimed him: "Today you will be with me in paradise."

Was that a healing? I believe it was. If opening a door of hope to a hopeless dying man is a healing of the spirit, then that was a healing from God, as truly a healing as the one my parents received from my sister's message in her New Testament.

I believe that God is the Great Improviser. When something terrible happens, God's heart is the first to break. And at that moment God says to himself and to us, "What new thing can we do now to turn this tragedy into an occasion of new hope?" If we can keep our minds and hearts open to God, I believe he will take us down that path to healing and new life.

Some people will say, understandably, "That is not good enough for me. If God, who is supposed to be omnipotent, cannot stop the tragedy from happening, He is not a good enough God for me. I will get along without him, thank you." But there is no God who bursts into our world to stop tragedies from happening. There is no such God that I know of. There is only a God who keeps turning death into life.

At home I have a book entitled, *Dying We Live*, a collection of letters from men and women who died in the concentration camps. They are an incredible testimony to the power of faith to sustain the victims to their last moments on earth. One wrote to his wife: "I trust and I pray. I have learned much in this rigorous year (in the camp). God has become more real and more immediate to me." When I first read that, I could not believe it. Such an expression of faith seemed to me to be naive, a childish faith, a denial of the horror. But the cumulative evidence of all those letters from men and women from every walk of life moved me deeply.

What is the healing path? It is not medicine, it is not psychotherapy, it is not the laying on of hands, it is not recovery of lost possessions or even the mending of bones and organs, though all these things may be part of the healing experience. I believe that the healing path is a *reunion*, a reunion of a lost soul and the soul's Maker; a reunion of a spiritual orphan and his heavenly Father and heavenly Mother; it is a coming home to God. All other healings apart from that reunion are partial.

In Jesus' story of the Prodigal Son, the boy goes off to a far country to separate from his family, to become his own man. You can't blame him, except that he's a little arrogant and rude about it as young people sometimes are when they are having trouble separating from a close parental relationship. The father understands. He doesn't argue; he lets him go, no strings, no little lectures, no packet of postcards to send home to Mother. He just lets him go. He knows that is what it is to be a father: to raise a son and then to let him go, to set him free to be himself. But the father's heart is in his throat. He knows it is a dangerous world out there.

Of course, as you know, the worst happens. Alone and broke, the son nearly dies in a famine, and is reduced to feeding pigs and also—to survive—eating the slop the pigs eat. Even in this short story, one can sense the boy's despair, his shame, and his loneliness. In the midst of his misery, the Bible says the young man "comes to himself," and he says, "I will arise and go to my father and I will say

to him, 'Here I am, a foolish son. Please take me back.'"
As you will remember, the father sees him coming a long
way off across the desert. He doesn't wait for the son to
come home and explain himself; he rushes out across the
desert and throws his arms around him, and cries out,
"Welcome home, my son, I have missed you. You may
have gone away but you never left my heart. Come, let's
celebrate!" It's a reunion, reconciliation.

Was that a healing? Certainly. It was a healing not just of a
father-son relationship; it was a healing of a son's despair,
of his shame, perhaps most importantly a healing of the
son's alienation from himself. He didn't get any of the
things he went off to the far country to get. But he got
something else that he did not realize he needed: he got
the love that he thought he didn't need any more. He
found not just a place to lay his head; he found his true
home.

I think that is the way it is with God and us. I believe
every healing path begins with the inward prayer, "I will
arise and go to my Father." In that instant God opens his
heart to us and claims us as his beloved child. And we are
home. Whatever mending *can* take place of our broken
bodies and broken hearts will happen there.

I also believe that sometimes there are worse things than
dying. When there is no hope of recovery and we are
faced with a long siege of pain and deterioration, maybe
the only way to get well is to die. If we have any faith in
the resurrection which we share with Christ, then there
must be healing in death.

In the months that I have been thinking about this
sermon, I have spoken to many for whom the subject of

healing is intensely relevant. Some are struggling with cancer. Some have been going through heartbreaking divorces. Some have lost children and parents. Some have been fighting crippling depressions. I knew that some of those with whom I spoke would probably be here this morning, and I have not known what I was going to say. It is hard to speak confidently of healing to those for whom the stakes are so high. I know there is no simple answer for any of them when I speak of God's healing. I do not know why God did not heal my sister. I do not know why God did not intervene to stop the Holocaust or the rape of Kosovo. There is so much that I do not know. But there are some things of which I am sure:

- I am sure that God never *punishes* us with sickness or with the loss of a loved one. Some Christians have made the outrageous claim that AIDS is God's punishment for homosexuality. I do not believe in such a God. No loving God would do that any more than a human parent would punish her children with sickness or with the loss of a loved companion.

- I am sure that God does not sprinkle miracles around from on high, curing a cancer here but not there, one broken relationship but not another, saving someone from an accident at one moment but not another. God would no more treat us that way than a human parent would treat his children in such a random and chaotic manner.

- I am sure that God does not wait to do good until she is asked, or until we get our prayers just right, any more than a human mother would withhold her protection from her children because they do not quite know how to ask for it.

For reasons I do not fully understand, God withholds himself from manipulating his creation, even for what would seem to us to be a just cause. But I do know that God sets a moral code at the center of human life and that the consequences of our violating it are inescapable. I do know that in a world characterized by free will there are accidents and failures that are not part of God's plan. Some misguided people said that the death of John F. Kennedy, Jr. must have been in some way the will of God. I don't believe it. I think that when the waters of Nantucket Sound closed over the plane that carried John Kennedy, his wife, Caroline, and her sister, Lauren, to their deaths, that God's heart was the first of all our hearts to break.

I do know that Christ rising from the dead overcame every threat to the human spirit and transformed the human tragedy into a journey of hope.

When we speak of healing, we are speaking not only of ourselves and our individual bodies and spirits, but we are speaking of God's world, which she loves. We are speaking of the healing of broken families, of estranged husbands and wives and lovers, of racial antagonisms, of wars between nations and tribes, violence in our schools, hatreds that fester in our society.

I am sure that God is the source of all healing in the universe and that God wants nothing more than that we receive it from her hand. About everything else I am unsure. The church's ministries of the laying on of hands and of the Eucharist give focus to God's call that all things be reunited and reconciled and made whole in God, that the broken be mended and that the lost be found and brought home. As we join in those sacramental acts, we are joined to the One whose love is our healing. So wherever you are on your journey of faith,

> if you have a physical illness,
> if you are frightened,
> if you are lost,
> if you are broken hearted,
> if you feel guilt or are ashamed,
> if your heart is sick because of the violence in the world,
> if you bring a prayer for someone else who is ill or in trouble,
> if someone you love has died…
>
> then say to yourself, as the boy did in the story, "I will arise and go to my Father."

And then come to the church's altar rail and open your heart to whatever healing God will give, trusting that *it is being given* though you may not yet understand how. Put aside for the moment your skepticism. Look into the heart of God who reaches out to touch you in the deep places of your heart.

And let the mystery of the Risen Christ settle upon your heart. He reaches out his arms to you; he welcomes you; he claims you as his own. You are home!

4

LOVING, LOSING AND LETTING GO

Three Talks On Bereavement and Loss

I. Love and Mourning

T o love another person is to face the possibility of losing the one we love. We all live by loving and losing and then letting go of the one we have lost. Because we *love*, our losing can be as painful as a hot knife in the belly, or it can be numbness and emptiness and the loss of a sense of purpose. This is the first of three talks on loving, losing and letting go. I have called this first talk, "Love and Mourning," and it is about bereavement, the loss of a love. Next week we will talk about transitions and the loss we feel when we leave something of ourselves behind as we go on to some new phase of life. The last talk will be about facing our own death, which is the ultimate experience of loving, losing and letting go.

I will be talking today mainly about mourning the death of *people* we love. But we may mourn in a similar way the loss of a marriage, or the coming apart of a special friendship, or even the loss of a pet. When my parents died, both in their eighties, they were diminished and ill and had lost any real interest in living. They died within six months of each other, and I conducted the funeral service for each of them. But I did not feel an acute sense of loss because in some sense I had lost them long before they died, and I grieved for them slowly over a long period of time. The sharpest pain of loss I can remember feeling in my life was when, as a ten-year-old child, I stood on the sidewalk and saw my beloved dog run over by a truck. I can still feel that as though it were yesterday. I am lucky that I have not had to go through the insupportable pain of losing a child or my wife. Those are surely the most painful losses of all.

As we shall see, mourning comes in different ways. But it does come inexorably for all of us, for to live is to lose. And to love is to lose painfully. The question is, how are we going to mourn? *For to mourn is to do honor, both to the one who has gone and to our own feelings.*

Most of you have read books on bereavement. They usually set forth a pattern of mourning, stages that a person typically goes through. Some of us find it annoying that some Julia Child of sorrow is trying to provide us with a step-by-step recipe for correct grief. But if we can hear about those steps not as something we *have* to go through, but simply as levels of experience which can help us understand what we are feeling, then we can accept the fact that, as C.S. Lewis wrote in *A Grief Observed*, "sorrow turns out to be not a state but a process."

I will describe a three-step process, as set forth by Judith Viorst in her landmark book, *Necessary Losses*.

The first step is *shock*. It is characterized by numbness and disbelief. It is incomprehensible to us that someone we love is suddenly just not there anymore, even if we have been expecting it. We may cry; or we may sit silently, overcome with the gravity of the moment. But our minds do not want to grasp the full reality.

Mark Twain's daughter died suddenly at the age of twenty-four. He writes of his benumbed disbelief:

> It is one of the mysteries of our nature that a man, all unprepared, can receive a thunderstroke like that and *live*. The intellect is stunned by the shock and but groping gathers the meaning of the words. The power to realize their full import is mercifully wanting. The mind has a dumb sense of vast loss—that is all. It will take mind and memory months and possibly years to gather the details and thus learn and know the whole extent of the loss.

Even when we know that a death is coming, we are never completely prepared for the actuality of it. I was in a hospital room when a man died after months of fighting a losing battle with cancer. His wife was sitting by the bed, as she had been every day. She suddenly looked up at me and said, "I think he has stopped breathing." I called the nurse, who put a stethoscope to his chest and confirmed that he was dead. The wife cried out to him, "No! No, you haven't left me. You haven't gone." Then she stood up and said, "What does a nurse know? We'll put a call in for the doctor. Meanwhile, let's let him sleep," and she left the room.

So, shock is the first stage. Then slowly the reality seeps in under the barrier of disbelief, and we begin the second and the longer phase of *intense psychic pain*. It is characterized by a confusing welter of feelings and non-feelings: weeping, emptiness, emotional swings, lethargy one moment and hyperactivity the next moment, hopelessness, anger. Helen Hayes described the two years following her husband's death in this way:

> "I was just as crazy as you can be and still be at large. I didn't have any really normal minutes during those two years. It wasn't just grief. It was total confusion. I was just nutty…"

It is not unusual to find ourselves getting *angry*: at the doctor, at God, at friends who are trying to comfort us, at our children who don't quite know how to be there in the right way, even at the one who died for leaving us. About twenty years ago I was facing a very grave illness, and Wendy said to me, when things looked very black, "Clarke, if you die I will be so angry at you! Don't you dare die!"

We are likely to feel some *guilt*, usually a mixture of reasonable and unreasonable guilt. When they were alive, we felt some ambivalence towards the ones we loved. We saw them as less than perfect and we loved them less than perfectly. We may even have fantasized what it would be like if they were dead. Now that they are gone we idealize them, and remonstrate against ourselves: "I should have been kinder, more understanding, more grateful; I should have tried harder. I shouldn't have gone home the night he died."

We may feel some relief when a person has died at the end of a long siege, and then feel guilty for feeling relieved.

Sometimes we are justified in feeling some guilt. In the last months of my beloved mother-in-law's life, I did not get over to the nursing home to see her very often. I rationalized that she was "out of it," that she would not know if I were there. But in my heart I knew that was only partly true. I just kept putting it off because I couldn't bear to see her in that condition or to feel so helpless. When the news of her death came, I was ashamed that I had let her slip away with so little attention, and I could hardly look her friends in the eye who had come to sit by her bed every day to hold her hand. My mourning for her was suffused with guilt.

We may go through times of such aching *longing* for the physical presence of the one who has died that we feel it in our bodies like a knife wound. We are sure we will never have a friend, a lover, a companion like that again. Despair and futility overwhelm us. A widowed husband told me the nights were the hardest, the bed was so empty. He kept reaching for her, and when he realized she wasn't there, he would hug the pillow and cry.

Each of us will go through this acute period of grief, some quietly, some more vocally. In our own different ways we will pass through the tears and the terrors, the anger and the guilt, the longing and the despair until we begin to come to the end of our mourning. Then we will move toward its completion. And though we will still have times of weeping, longing, and missing, we will find some degree of *acceptance, recovery and adaptation.* This is the third phase.

We *accept* the fact that the dead will not return, that pain will come and go, that troubling dreams will sometimes haunt our sleep, but that there are new things in our life that deserve our best attention and energy. Acceptance is not the same as grim resignation. It is a letting go of what we cannot recover, and reaching out for some things that are new and fresh and challenging.

We *recover* our stability, our energy, our hopefulness and our capacity to enjoy and invest in life again.

We *adapt* to altered circumstances. We modify the picture we have of our lives, our expectations, our self-definitions. This is more than just making the best of a bad situation. It is creative change: new goods, new kinds of pleasures. They may seem trivial, even contrived at first, but they can grow into major new satisfactions.

But this process is not a straight-line process from here to there. It is more like a corkscrew. It keeps doubling back upon itself so that just when you think you are over some particularly painful memory, you get a whiff of something that smells like his pipe tobacco or after-shave lotion, and you look around to see if he isn't there, or you hear a creak on the stair at the moment she often came home, and for a wild moment you think it is she returning.

C.S. Lewis wrote, following the death of his wife:

How often—will it be for always?—how often will the vast emptiness astonish me like a complete novelty and make me say, "I never realized my loss till this moment?" The same leg is cut off time after time. The first plunge of the knife into the flesh is felt again and again. One keeps on emerging from a phase, but it always recurs. "Round and round. Everything repeats. Am I going in circles?"

Sometimes it seems that way, especially at anniversary times, and when we revisit places that we once visited together. But in spite of setbacks and recurrences, *there is an end to mourning*. Here are some excerpts from a daughter's record of mourning for her mother, *A Book about My Mother*, by Toby Talbot.

I awake in the middle of the night and tell myself, She's gone. My mother is dead. Never will I see her again. How to grasp this? ...

Oh, Mama, I don't want to eat, to walk, to get out of bed. Reading, working, cooking, listening, mothering. Nothing matters. I do not want to be distracted from my grief. I wouldn't mind dying. I wouldn't mind at all. I wake from sleep in the middle of every night and say to myself, "My mother is dead!"

Mourning... . You seem to be filled with it. Always. In a sense, like pregnancy. But ... pregnancy imparts a sense of doing something even while inactive, whereas mourning bequeaths a sense of futility and meaninglessness in the midst of activity...Her death is the only thing on my mind.

It's all a rotten hoax, this life of ours. You go from zero to zero. Why attach yourself to love only to have your beloved ripped from you? The upshot of love is pain. Life is a death sentence. Better not to give yourself to anything...

Am I healing? I'm able to gaze at her photograph without that tourniquet tightening round my throat, clamping memory...I'm beginning to see her in *her* life, and not only myself, bereft of her.

Piece by piece, I reenter the world. A new phase. A new body, a new voice. Birds console me by flying, trees by growing, dogs by the warm patch they leave on the sofa, unknown people merely by performing their motions. It's like a slow recovery from a sickness, this recovery of one's self... My mother was at peace. She was ready. A free woman. "Let me go," she said. Okay, Mama, I'm letting you go.

Toward the end of her book, Talbot says that as she is gaining her freedom from her mother's physical presence she is "being filled with her as never before." In this way she is describing a process that psychoanalysts call "internalization." Therapists say that it is by internalizing the dead, by making them part of our inner world, that we can at last complete the mourning process. That is the way an infant comes to trust that his mother who leaves the room has not abandoned him. The infant's anxiety is soothed when he is able to hold onto an inner experience of his mother when his mother is not visible. It is an important step in the development of the infant's psyche. Judith Viorst comments further:

> ... while the touch is gone, the laugh is gone,
> the promise and the possibilities are gone,
> the sharing of music and wine and bed is
> gone—it is true nonetheless that by making
> the dead a part of our inner world, we in
> some important ways never lose them.

You may say, as one recently widowed woman did, "I liked what I had. I don't want anything else. I want back what I had." That may be absolutely true. But you have a choice: to stay stuck in that painful groove, or to allow yourself to move beyond it. Internalization is part of the process of moving on. Your life may not be what you want, but it is still hopeful in its own way, rich in its own way.

Not to let go, not to move on is to leave yourself vulnerable to a host of ills, both psychological and physical. The death of a love is the most stressful event you will encounter in your life. Survivors statistically are at a higher risk to die, or to kill themselves, or to become ill, or have accidents, or to overindulge in smoking, drinking, and drugs, or to suffer from depression. A woman whose husband's death left her seeing the future as "a big black hole" had to consciously decide to keep going; it was an act of the will. "I had to decide every morning that I would live," she said. We may unconsciously choose the other way; we may unconsciously choose to die, and then we will slip away both mentally and physically.

What can we do to make our way through grief in a reasonably hopeful and healthy way? There is no formula that works for everyone. But clinical experience suggests that there are some guiding principles that generally help. I have reduced them to some do's and don'ts:

- *Do* be prepared for a painful struggle, and do know that it *will* end.

- *Do* give yourself time. Not that "time heals all wounds;" time doesn't necessarily do that. But think of it as healing "in your own time." For some it takes much longer than others for reasons you have no control over.

- *Do* participate actively and intentionally in your recovery instead of waiting passively for the pain to stop and the curtain of grief to lift.

- *Don't* isolate. How easy it is to retreat into your dark corner of pain and to resist all invitations, insisting there is nothing you really want to do. You may not want to do much of anything, but select some things and do them anyway.

- *Don't* rely too much on others, either. Friends and activities shouldn't distract you completely from the solitude in which you need to work out the meaning of your aloneness.

- *Don't* make big decisions or plans, like moving or entering into a new permanent relationship. Wait for emotional recovery for those changes. But do make small decisions and plans: take trips, make social plans, try out new hobbies. The more concrete and specific you can be, the more quickly you will find stability.

- *Do* talk about your mourning process with those who care about you. Shakespeare wrote, "Give sorrow words; the grief that does not speak Whispers the o'er fraught heart, and bids it break."

- *Do* have a sense of humor about what you are going through, even though at times that will seem impossible. Humor greases the wheels of heaviness. At one point during the illness that I mentioned earlier, Wendy cried out impulsively, "If you die on me, I'm through with you!" We both realized what she said at the same moment and broke out laughing. We laughed and giggled together for twenty minutes.

- *Do* allow yourself to experience as deeply and richly as you can the feelings that come and go, both the painful ones and the happier ones. That is hard because most of us have been taught that painful feelings are somehow bad and should be suppressed lest they be a burden to others. Or we may fear that if we let the painful feelings emerge they will overwhelm us, and we will have a breakdown. Healing comes from facing deep feelings and working them through.

- *Do* hold on tenaciously to your faith. God will seem to disappear during the most painful times, and you will feel angry and betrayed by God. C. S. Lewis writes in *A Grief Observed*, "Where is God? ...turn to him (when you are happy) with gratitude and praise, and you will be—or so it feels— welcomed with open arms. But go to him when your need is desperate, when all other help is vain, and what do you find? A door slammed in your face, a sound of bolting and double bolting on the inside. After that, silence. You may as well turn away."

· C.S. Lewis made his way back to a renewed sense of God by simply holding on and not letting go, though his faith was never quite as tidy and glossy as it had been before. That will be so for you, too, if you do not let your anger at God and your transient atheism drive you into spiritual exile.

· Finally, *do* keep praying whether it feels good and helpful or not. Keep up the habit. As St. Paul said, "Be constant in prayer." It will be a lonely experience at first. But know that it is your pain that is blocking out a sense of God's presence, not his absence, as gray sky blocks out the ever-burning sun. Let your prayers be simple and honest; invite God into the darkest, messiest corners of your heart, especially that corner where you have tossed your shriveled-up soul. Invite God to see and share your pain and confusion. Don't forget, he has seen them before! Then ask God to lead you by the hand to new places, greener, livelier, more serene, into a place of light. And in your time and his, he will. This is your healing path.

Mourning is not negative. To mourn is to do honor both to the one who is gone and to our own feelings. The depth of our mourning is the measure of the greatness of our love.

Let us pray:

> God of Wonder...
> Giver of Life...
> Energize us so that...
> Our faith may give us the vision and the mission;
> Our hope may give us spirit and energy;
> Our love may be grounded in the miracle of your love.
> Sustain us in the pain of our losses.
> Be with us as we continue our walk into the future with an open heart
> So that we will discover a new future,
> A new life,
> Because we have become fertile again.
> As Isaiah prayed...
> "See, I am doing something new...
> even now it comes to Light; can you not see it?"
> Let us go forth now in gentleness, peace and joy.
> Through Jesus Christ, Our Lord.
> Amen

II. Growing a New Self

In Part I, "Love and Mourning," I talked about bereavement—the loss of a love, or a close friend, or a life-companion. We tried to understand that everyone grieves these losses, usually painfully. No two people grieve in the same way, but for all of us grieving is a process that takes time, patience and a willingness to trust the healing power of God.

We are never the same after such a loss. There is an empty chair at the table, an empty place in our bed, a missing companion on our walks and at our dinner parties. It is as though a limb had been torn from our body. There is a tear in the flesh that can slowly heal but leaves a scar; a missing limb can be compensated for but not replaced. In time the pain diminishes or the numbness gives way to sensation and we learn to live a different kind of life. It takes courage and faith, but there is an end to mourning.

Now I want to talk about a different kind of loss—the loss of ourselves, the loss of our sense of identity, when changes occur in our lives and force us to give up the way we have seen ourselves before and to redefine ourselves. We have to deal with changing images of ourselves. These changes may also be painful, and we need to mourn the passing of our former selves, of unrealized hopes, and shattered dreams and, as we grow older, the loss of physical beauty and power.

As with bereavement, these changes often bring with them a sense of shock, disappointment, fear, even anger, and shame. And almost always they bring with them the misapprehension that because we aren't what we used to be we are not what we ought to be.

For example, a woman struggles to find herself after a painful divorce, and must recover from the death of her dream of a happy marriage. She must find a new identity as a single mother, something she had never before contemplated.

A middle-aged man is passed over for a promotion that he has worked towards for years and he sees his career hopes slipping away. He must redefine himself and find new ways to affirm who he is.

A woman looks in the mirror and contemplates the significance of the sagging flesh under her chin; she will never be young again. She has to think of her beauty and power in new ways.

Judith Viorst writes:

> What am I doing with a mid-life crisis?
> This morning I was seventeen.
> I have barely begun the beguine and it's good night ladies
> Already.

> While I have been wondering who to be
> When I grow up someday,

> My acne has vanished away and it's
> Sagging kneecaps
> Already.

> When did the boys I once clung to
> Start losing their hair?
> Why can't I take barefoot walks in the park
> Without giving my kidneys a chill?
> There's poetry left in me still and it
> Doesn't seem fair.

> While I was thinking I was just a little girl
> My future turned into my past.
> The time for wild kisses goes fast and it's
> Time for Sanka

> Already.

Or, as another poet put it:

When I was young and miserable and pretty
And poor, I'd wish
What all girls wish: to have a husband,
A house and children. Now that I'm old, my wish
Is womanish;
That the boy putting groceries in my car
See me. It bewilders me that he doesn't see me.

The loss of an attractive self-image, a familiar and comfortable pattern of living, or a hoped-for success leads almost inevitably to some degree of depression. Depression is not necessarily a bad thing. It is simply a sign that we are going through a process of disorientation, with the attendant feelings of confusion and fear. The question is not whether we will be depressed; the question is how long will it last? How disabling will it be? And the question is how solid and satisfying will be the new me that emerges from the scattered pieces of the old me?

Every life change involves loss, as well as the possibility of a new gain. Psychologists tell us that any loss—of a loved one or of a pattern of living—involves not just the loss of that person or that familiar structure, but also a profound disruption of our identity, of our sense of who we are, a numbing sense of disorganization of the self.

Psychiatrist Frederic Flach wrote a book called *The Secret Strength of Depression*. In it he argues persuasively that we need to learn the fine art of falling apart. That involves our accepting the chaotic feelings that go with depression as normal and natural, just as a wound is a normal and natural result of a trauma. Normal depression is frequently part of the grieving process.

We are talking about learning to let go of an image of ourselves that cannot be recovered, that must be replaced with a new image of ourselves, without self-reproach, with imagination and courage and faith.

I'll give you an example from Wendy's and my personal life. Our three children all left home at the age of thirteen. That may seem odd, but we were living in New York City at the time and they went off to boarding schools. One day, our daughter asked Wendy, "Mom, now that we're gone from the house, what are you going to do with the rest of your life?" We laughed at our fourteen-year-old daughter's grown-up question, but it came as a shock to Wendy, who was only thirty-nine years old. I remember her feeling ashamed at being sad, at not having a ready answer, at not, in fact, having any idea what her life could look like without the kids at home. I remember her unexpected and embarrassing floods of tears. I did not understand her pain and she did not understand my not understanding, even though she didn't understand it herself.

Meanwhile, we noticed that we were quarrelling and picking on each other with increasing frequency. But it never occurred to us that our irritability and impatience with each other might have something to do with our children's departure. If we had understood that, we might have been able to offer each other a wiser love to soothe the pain of our transition. We could have encouraged each other to express the pain we each felt at our changing roles as parents. But we had never been taught to grieve that kind of loss.

Just as we can grieve the loss of a past identity, we can grieve the loss of a future one, a cherished hope.

For example, Ben and Madeleine (not their real names) came in to see me when their three-year-old marriage had come to a crisis point. Ben was a highly artistic young man and had planned to become a commercial artist. He fell in love with his college classmate, Madeleine, and their plan was to get married after graduation. Madeleine would work while he attended art school and then start his career. However, Madeleine became pregnant.

They did not believe in abortion, so Ben abandoned his plans for art school. They were married and Ben got a job selling life insurance. He hated his job but he was actually quite successful. He didn't tell Madeleine of his deep disappointment at having to give up his dream of becoming an artist. He believed it would be unfair to burden her with his unhappiness. He thought, "If I just ignore my feelings and don't think about it, there won't be any problem."

But as time went on, he became more withdrawn, more rigid and more irritable. He was a harsh father and a critical husband, though always maintaining what he thought was a positive and dutiful manner. Nothing Madeleine did seemed to please him any more. She finally insisted that they go for counseling.

In the first session, Ben focused on Madeleine's inadequacies which seemed to me to be exaggerated. So I saw Ben alone in the second session. I suggested that he sit back and close his eyes and tell me whatever came into his mind. The only thing he wasn't to talk about was Madeleine.

He was silent a long time, and then began somewhat haltingly to talk about his lost dream of being an artist. As he told me about it he began to cry, and for half an hour he sobbed. When I asked what Madeleine knew about his deep feelings, he explained that he had kept his feelings to himself so as not to burden her and maybe destroy their chances for happiness together.

Very gently I encouraged Ben to begin little by little to let Madeleine understand his pain. To his surprise, Madeleine was much more compassionate and more intuitive than he had given her credit for. She had always known about his disappointment but had been unable to get him to talk to her about it.

Ben's behavior became softer and their warm feelings of love for one another began to come back. Together they began to look ahead to a time when he could take art courses and plan for a change in careers. Meanwhile, Ben found opportunities to do more creative and artistic work for his company's advertising department. His creativity, which had been blocked by his repressed anger, began to blossom. Today, with three children and a strong marriage, Ben is head of the advertising department of his company and maintains a small practice as a freelance commercial artist.

The point is that Ben never allowed himself to mourn the loss of his dream, and to let Madeleine share that process with him. He never knew how to do that, never knew that it was permitted to him as a dutiful husband to share his disappointment with his wife. Not only did he imagine that it would crush her, but he thought she would think him weak and pathetic. In reality, the reverse was true. Also, she had her own disappointments and guilt that he knew nothing about.

We are talking about losing and letting go of an image of oneself, of a sense of identity. It is a kind of grieving. Usually the word grieving brings to mind being mournful, melancholy, dwelling on sorrow, maybe feeling sorry for ourselves, maybe being a little self-indulgent. I happen to think that a little self-pity is appropriate. Who wouldn't feel sorry for himself when he has suffered a painful loss? But after a while we need to shift our focus to recovery and see ourselves as engaged in a transition to something new.

Let's define "grieving." By "grieving" I mean being open and receptive to feelings inside us that are painful or sorrowful or angry, listening to them with sympathy for ourselves. I also mean allowing these feelings, which we are usually ashamed of, to become part of the rich mix of our emotions rather than clamping down on them. And I mean finding ways to talk about our feelings with some people we trust who can help us to move on. Grief is not shameful!

The failure to grieve can have long-term effects.

A young woman named Mary came to me complaining of depression and uncontrollable anger and a series of failed relationships. She grew up the only child of an alcoholic father and an immature, dependent mother. As a young child she was the responsible one in her chaotic family; she was the balance wheel that made her family work. She resented that role, and quit school in tenth grade and went to work, primarily to get away from her family.

I helped her to begin the mourning process which she had never allowed herself to go through. She began to get in touch with her rage at her mother who had never really been a mother to her, her ambivalent feelings for her father whom she loved even though he had often abandoned her in alcoholic stupors, and her sadness for the little kid she had been who had never had a childhood. These were severe losses for her. She needed to bring her feelings about them into awareness so she could begin to accept them and make them a part of the conscious pattern of her adult life.

Once she understood that depression was a natural response to the profound disappointments and losses of her childhood, her depression began to lift. She initiated some helpful conversations with her father which brought them closer together, and she painfully accepted the fact that her mother would never be the mother she yearned for. Mary's grieving process continued for many months, growing less and less painful. She gave me one of my most helpful definitions of grieving: grieving is learning to accept, even to love the hidden parts of ourselves. In Mary's case, the hidden parts were her anger at her parents that she was supposed to love—and in fact did love, her guilt at leaving the family, and her deep sadness at the loss of her childhood.

As long as we think of painful feelings as negative, we will want to repress them. As long as we repress them, we cannot think about them. And as long as we cannot think about them, we cannot make choices about them.

George Regas, Rector Emeritus of All Saints Church in Pasadena, California, famously begins every sermon with the words, "O God, make us masters of ourselves, that we may become servants of others..." It is a noble sentiment, but how can we become masters of what we do not know? How can we know what we do not allow ourselves to feel? How can we become servants of others if we do not listen with kindness to ourselves?

Let's face it! Our culture discourages mourning, even forbids it except for brief periods of time. We are taught instead to be optimistic and up-beat, to hide our disappointments, fears and sorrows. So we are working against strong prohibitions when we say we must learn to listen to our painful feelings and embrace them.

Learning to embrace the hidden parts of ourselves, the darker colors in our emotional rainbow, is the pathway to wholeness. It isn't simple, but we can learn to do it. It takes practice. Those who love us can help us by listening to us without judging, without trying to "hurry up" our grieving.

A young man I know wrote a letter to his father to thank him for helping him to trust his feelings as he was growing up. It is a beautiful letter about a lovely father-son relationship. The father shared it with me. In his "Dear Dad" letter, the son wrote in part:

> ...in our many lengthy discussions, when typically you would fire up your pipe after the first five or ten minutes and settle in for the marathon, I recall that I did most of the talking. You did the listening, never anxious to jump in, give advice, chastise, direct, judge. You let me explore my own often frightening feelings. In this loving act of listening you taught me how to listen to myself, to respect the signals my feelings were sending and eventually to be able to listen effectively to other...

...Through many of our conversations you enabled me to develop my own language to express myself, not fearing criticism, to seek the truth about myself and to discern the message being sent by my gut. And through it all my anxiety waned and my insight grew and my sense of myself gradually solidified. What a gift you have given me!

The father told me how deeply touched he was by his son's letter; especially since, in the midst of his own personal struggle to acknowledge his own feelings, he was not aware he had given that gift to his son. Thus it is that as we try to learn the art of mourning our losses, unwittingly we help those we love to do the same.

During my years on the staff of All Saints Church as Associate for Pastoral Care, I counseled twenty or thirty women who were trying to cope with the shock of mastectomy. The loss of the feeling of attractiveness, of desirability, in each case was almost overwhelming. After a while I realized how essential it was for women going through a mastectomy to be able to express their fears and to talk about how they might recover emotionally from the devastating change in the way they felt about themselves. I recruited several of the most beautiful and elegant women in the congregation who had had mastectomies to call on our mastectomy patients in the hospital. They were living examples that mastectomies do not destroy a woman's attractiveness. Then we started a group that met regularly in which women could support each other in recovery and self-acceptance. It was an essential aid to mourning their loss and visualizing their future.

Some of my friends who have been through a divorce tell me that divorce can be the most devastating of all life changes; in some ways it can be even more painful than losing a spouse by death. Because, not only do they go through all the agonies of a bereavement, but they have to endure the added pain of rejection and the accusation of failure at one of life's most elemental roles—that of wife or husband. How is it possible that a person could go through such an experience without getting depressed? It isn't a question of whether you will get depressed, but of how long, and of how crippling, and of how soon can you trust the new you that emerges from the scattered pieces of the old you? It is a question of how you will deal with the inevitable feelings of shame and rage and rejection, and finally let them go.

Letting go takes courage. It also requires a good deal of faith. We usually think of faith as a strong belief in the power of God, but that is only part of faith. The other part of faith is the ability to feel, albeit imperfectly, that with all our faults and failures we are worthy of respect and love.

We cannot create faith; we can only receive it. It is a gift given to us through love. When someone loves us in spite of our failures and faults, they give us an inexplicable gift of affirmation. When we experience God's love we receive that gift of affirmation, not just from another fallible human being who, after all, might be wrong, but from The One who is the very author of life itself. We will think of all kinds of reasons to refuse God's love, because we are so sure that we are guilty of something that forbids it, but God gives her love steadily. As we let God share our grieving, we let her into the hidden places. Beginning there, she brings us love and renewal, hope and new life. Faith is trust in the power of God, and it is trust in our own worth inexplicably affirmed by the miracle of God's love.

Faith unlocks our creativity. Remember how Ben's creativity began to blossom when he accepted his disappointment as natural and began to share it with Madeleine? Our past may slip away from us, our future may change, our bodies may age. But our creativity never grows old. It just gets blocked by repressed anger, fear and sadness. We are creative when we visualize ourselves in new ways and sense new possibilities in ourselves, try out new things, make mistakes, have a sense of humor about our fallibility, enjoy small pleasures.

These are all things that God wants for us. He will give them to us if we meet him in the place of our hidden feelings and let him take us with him to new adventures of living.

Let us pray:

God of Wonder...
Giver of Life...
Energize us so that...
Our faith may give us the vision and the mission;
Our hope may give us spirit and energy;
Our love may be grounded
in the miracle of your love.
Sustain us in the pain of our losses.
Be with us as we continue our walk into the future
with an open heart
So that we will discover a new future,
A new life,

Because we have become fertile again.
As Isaiah prayed,
"See, I am doing something new...
Even now it comes to Light; can you not see it?"
Let us go forth now in gentleness, peace, and joy.
Through Jesus Christ, Our Lord.

Amen.

III. "As Dying and Behold We Live!"

After hearing my first talk on bereavement, someone told me he was dismayed that I would speak of the death of a pet as the most painful loss that I had experienced. What I said was that my parents were greatly diminished when they died, so I grieved for them slowly over a long period of time even before they died. When they did die, I did not feel the acute pain that I felt when I saw my beloved dog killed by a truck before my eyes when I was ten years old. Even though that was sixty years ago, I can still feel some of that pain as though it were yesterday. I was illustrating the point that there is not just one correct hierarchy of grief, not just one way of experiencing loss; we grieve in many different ways.

Nevertheless, I understand that person's feeling. I know that he had recently lost a son in a shooting accident. It points up how difficult this subject is to talk about. I know there are some here this morning who are in the midst of grief, and who will find whatever I say inadequate to their pain. To them I apologize in advance if what I say does not seem to do justice to their suffering.

This is the third and final talk in the series entitled "Loving, Losing and Letting Go." The first talk was on bereavement, the loss of a loved family member or friend. The second talk was about life transitions, which also involve loss—not of a person, but of a sense of self, a sense of identity, when we have to redefine ourselves after a divorce, the loss of a job, or even the loss of a cherished dream of the future.

It is time now to talk about our own dying. It is the ultimate loss that we will experience, the loss of our very existence, and often the loss of our dignity in the process. It is a difficult subject because there are some here who have had your own brush with death, indeed may still be close to that soul-shaking experience. Let me tell you about my brush with death.

In 1978 I was operated on for what was diagnosed as pancreatic cancer. The surgeon performed a bile-duct by-pass and sewed me up, and told Wendy to take me home and get my affairs in order because he estimated that I had about six months to live. Well, I am one of the lucky ones who recovered from that terrible illness, either because it was misdiagnosed or because I had an unexplained remission of the disease.

I remember the days and nights following the operation with awesome clarity; it was a time of emotional and spiritual desolation. I was in the dark valley overshadowed by death. The worst of it was that I was unable to pray or to feel any sense of God's comfort. My prayers turned to dust in my mouth; I would say the words and feel nothing but despair. It was very frightening; it was also very humiliating. After all, I was supposed to be the spiritual counselor of others; yet there I was, helpless when faced with my own spiritual loneliness.

I knew that my friends and family were praying for me. I had no choice but to lie back and rest in their prayers. You may remember the story in the Bible of the young man who was paralyzed and could not get to Jesus for healing. So his friends put him on a stretcher and carried him to Jesus; they had to let him down through a hole in the roof because they couldn't get through those who were crowding around him. That is what I felt like—a helpless man carried to the feet of Jesus by the persistent prayers of my friends. Their prayers were my only solace; they meant everything to me.

One night shortly after the operation, I felt touched by God. In the middle of the night, I was lying awake when in the deepest place of my heart I heard God whisper that I was going to be all right. I did not take that to mean that I was going to get well, only that it didn't matter. If I got well I would be all right, and if I died I would be all right. Either way I would be safe in God's care and life would go on. I felt the most immeasurable sense of peace. Was it really God speaking to me? Do we ever know that for certain? All I can tell you is that it changed my life. Since then I have known a serenity in that deep place of my heart that no human being could give me. So you need to know that it is in the context of that experience that I speak to you about facing our own death.

Many people tell me that they are not afraid of death, but it is the prospect of dying with its suffering and indignities that they are terrified of. They say they are at peace about the prospect of leaving this life and embarking on a new one. "I am not afraid of death," Woody Allen once said; "I just do not want to be there when it happens."

As Christians, we share with each other our love and worship of a Lord who died on a cross. And we hold to the belief that he rose from the dead, which makes it easier for us to look squarely at the reality of death. If our Savior can die, perhaps it isn't such a terrible thing for us to die. And if our Savior rose from the dead, then maybe it is reasonable for us to hope that we too will rise from death to new life. So the Christian story in which we are immersed has at its very center the reality of death and resurrection.

Not so for the culture in which we live. Our culture finds the idea of death to be almost intolerable, and tries to deny death by many forms of evasion and camouflage. Many American Christians evade the painful center of our faith. We wear little gold crosses, not as reminders of the death and resurrection of our Savior, or of the ambiguity of Christian experience, but as good luck charms. We are likely to read the Bible as a manual for personal success rather than the story of God's agony and faithfulness to us in spite of our faithlessness, our selfishness and spiritual pride. The idea that death is central to our faith seems to us an unwelcome and morbid intrusion upon our hard won optimism.

It is not that we totally deny the fact that men and women, including ourselves, are mortal. In fact we pride ourselves on the array of books, articles, seminars and TV shows which feature the fashionable subject of Dying and Death. But despite all that attention and all the talk, we go about our lives with the fact of our own death held at emotional bay. Denial of death means never allowing ourselves to confront the anxiety stirred by the prospect of this last separation.

You may well ask, "What's so bad about that? Who wants to think about dying? Who wants to be reminded that we go through our days and nights with an abyss of nothingness yawning under our feet?"

Freud said that denial of death is an impoverishment of life because it is the knowledge of life's fragility that gives it its value.

The great psychologist, Abraham Maslow, had a near-fatal heart attack. Following that devastating experience, he wrote in a letter:

> The confrontation with death, and the
> reprieve from it, makes everything so
> precious, so sacred, so beautiful, that I feel
> more strongly than ever the impulse to love
> life, to embrace it and to let myself be
> overwhelmed by it.
>
> Death, and its ever-present possibility,
> makes love, passionate love, more possible.
> I wonder if we could love passionately, if
> ecstasy would be possible at all, if we knew
> we would never die.

That is the significance of the breaking of a glass at a Jewish wedding: that pain is inevitable in every loving relationship; that life itself is fragile and can be broken in an instant.

Similarly, in the Christian Eucharist, when the celebrant breaks the bread it is a reminder of Christ's brokenness on the cross, a further reminder of how close our lives are to death at every minute, and of our hope for restoration when we too are raised with Christ in our joyful resurrection.

The wonderful movie, *Shadowlands*, tells the story of C.S. Lewis' marriage late in life to Joy, and of her death from cancer just three years later. At one point in the story, Joy admonishes him that he has been avoiding the subject of her dying, and that they must talk to each other openly about it; they cannot avoid it. She says, "Our pain now is part of our joy later." She means that the two things are inseparable. There can be no reality to their joy if it does not include the pain of her dying.

It is easy to philosophize about dying. But when we have our noses right up against the window of death, we may find the terror of the endless night overtaking us. Then we suddenly wake up to the fact that life is not a rehearsal.

The author Judith Viorst in a brief period of a few weeks lost her mother, a teen-aged neighbor, and a best friend. She wrote with great feeling, "Treach me how to know death and go on with life; teach me how to love life and not fear death; teach me, before it is time to take the final exam, the ABC of dying."

Death does seem to be a denial of life. It does seem to bring down to zero our sense of personal significance, and to render all of our achievements meaningless. It does seem to mock us. Is there one of us who can say that we have not at some moment been terrified at the thought of annihilation, or of going into the unknown? Is there one of us who has not pondered uneasily the question of how we will pay for our sins in the next life?

In Leo Tolstoy's classic short story "The Death of Ivan Ilych," Ivan Ilych cries out when he realizes that he is dying:

> My God! My God! ...I'm dying; ...it may
> happen this moment. There was light and
> now there is darkness. I was here and now
> I'm going there! There will be nothing...
> Can this be dying? No, I don't want to!

He is petrified. But the worst part for Ivan Ilych is that nobody will talk to him about it. They all pretend to his face that he is not dying at all. Tolstoy writes:

> Those lies—lies enacted over him on the
> eve of his death and destined to degrade
> this awful, solemn act... were a terrible
> agony for Ivan Ilych. He wanted to cry out,
> "Stop lying! You know and I know that I
> am dying. Then at least stop lying about it."

I want to share with you the stories of three women who shared their dying with me when I was the Associate for Pastoral Care at All Saints Church in Pasadena. Frannie (I am not using their real names) fought fiercely against her death until the moment she closed her eyes. Susan, facing an increasingly disfiguring cancer of the face, chose to commit suicide. Dorothy faced her death head on with supreme confidence in all that lay ahead for her. In her own way, each faced her death courageously and forthrightly.

Frannie came to me to ask if there was anything to faith healing. She had not been a churchgoer, but she had started coming to church at the age of thirty-eight because she was suffering from an advanced stage of cancer.

Though she wasn't sure she believed much of it, she said, "I like it. It is peaceful, and there is beauty here and kind people. It is a healing environment." She said she intended to beat the cancer, that there were many people who had unexplained remissions and reversals and she intended to be one of them.

Frannie was an expert tennis player. She continued to play tennis until her strength would not permit her to play any more. Then she put her racket on the shelf, as she said, "for the time being," and turned her attention to other pursuits. She signed up for a class in poetry writing, and joined a volunteer group at a shelter for the homeless. She put all of her personal affairs in order very methodically. "I am going to beat this thing," she said, a little defensively, "but there is no point in being sloppy about it. I might get hit by a truck tomorrow!"

One night, Frannie invited a group of her closest friends for dinner—about a dozen people. She told them that, since she lived alone, she would need the help of her friends if she became incapacitated. She passed out a list of the kind of things she might need from them and then asked each one in turn what he or she would like to do for her. No one was to offer to do anything he or she did not feel up to, and no one was to feel guilty about not doing what someone else was doing. But she needed to be able to count on each one if the fateful moment came when she could not take care of herself. She did not want to have to phone any of them and wonder if she was asking too much. Some would run errands, some would bring food, some would stay with her at night, some would help with intimate personal needs. She got them all organized. "Some of us do survive," she told them. "Now that this is taken care of, I can relax and devote all my energy to fighting for my life. I've played some tough matches in my life; this is the toughest."

She maintained a keen interest in all her friends, making daily phone calls all over, asking about them and their lives, scarcely mentioning her own illness.

Frannie believed until the very end that if a person really tried, the human spirit would triumph over biology. She came to church quite regularly right up to the end of her life. She always said that it helped her and she knew Jesus was on her side. I went to see her on the last day. She was so weak she could barely whisper. When I arrived, she handed me a small envelope with a note in it for me. In writing that was barely legible she had written, "OK, Clarke. Now it's your serve." Frannie died that night. Several close friends were with her, and it was a peaceful dying. She was ready to move on.

The second woman, Susan, was in her mid-fifties when they found cancer in her face. She was a handsome woman with a devoted husband and grown children. She had been a faithful church member for many years. She came to see me for pastoral support and we talked about the prospect of dying. She and I had similar views of the life to come, and we found it easy to talk and laugh together. We read C.S. Lewis' *The Great Divorce*, a book about life after death which had had a profound influence on me as a young man. It helped us both. It provided us with a common language and vision of what it may be like to continue on life's journey in the next world, being drawn ever closer to the throne of Grace.

Susan and her husband pursued every possible avenue of treatment for several years, even going to Mexico and South America for treatments that are not legal in America. While there were brief remissions, the cancer progressed. Painful lesions opened in her mouth and on her cheek. Then one day she came to me and said, "I'm going to die on Sunday. Do you think that is a terrible thing for me to do? I want your blessing." She described how she and her husband had gathered the necessary ingredients for what she called a "cocktail." She had met with each of her children individually, and while they had widely differing reactions to what she proposed, they all agreed in the end to support her and not to try to stop her.

I knew Susan to be a fighter. In this moment she determined not to let the cancer have the last word, to ravage her further or to inflict insupportable suffering upon her and her family. She chose not to let death take her, but to meet it at a time of her own choosing.

I have always believed that a person has a moral right to choose the time and the means of his or her dying. It is a highly controversial subject, and many of my friends disagree with me. I also believe that to make a decision for suicide takes courage and should be taken only after all resources for treatment have been exhausted. Over the years of my ministry, very few people have made the choice that Susan did. Most have chosen to display their courage by living out the struggle against debilitating illness.

So Susan told me she planned to go to church on Sunday morning with her husband and her children; then she would have a lovely dinner at home with them and in the afternoon she would retire to her bedroom for a nap. She would drink the cocktail, and she and her husband would curl up together on the bed as they had done a thousand times before. That is exactly what happened. I had a call that evening from her husband telling me that Susan had died peacefully, "in her sleep."

Susan died many years ago, but I have kept in my heart all these years the spiritual wholeness of her dying—her exhaustive pursuit of treatment, the counseling, our talks, the reading and laughing, the sharing with her family, the final morning in church, and the intimate gathering at home. I cannot believe that God frowned upon her final act.

There are some who would not choose suicide, but who greet death with open arms—"Sister Death," as St. Francis used to call it. The third woman, Dorothy, used to call the death she knew was imminent "another of God's miracles."

Dorothy was in her seventies. She had three children, all married, and a gaggle of grandchildren. Her husband loved her and gave her every possible measure of support in her last months.

When I went to see her, her hair was gone from the chemotherapy and she was in pain. She brightly asked me to sit down and help her plan her funeral. She couldn't remember the names of all the hymns she was considering (except "The Blue Green Hills of Earth," which was her personal favorite), so we hummed and stumbled our way through twenty hymns, laughing, trying out the tunes and words to see if they were what she wanted: "Oh, that one's no good. It's too serious!" or "Oh, I like that one. It feels like a celebration." Then we went over who would read what and say what, and what she wanted me to say about her. She said, "Don't mention my ex-husband or I'll fly down from the rafters and beat you with my wings!"

Suddenly tears would overtake her, waves of sadness at the thought of leaving her family and of the pain her death would cause her husband, which she could already see in his eyes. She would lie back on her pillows, her body heaving with grief, and I could do nothing but hold her hand.

I saw her frequently during those last months. Sometimes she would ask me to read the fourteenth chapter of St. John:

> Let not your heart be troubled; ye believe in
> God, believe also in me...In my Father's
> house are many mansions...I go to prepare a
> place for you ...and I will come again and
> receive you unto myself, that where I am
> there ye may be also.

She made me read it over and over to her, and she would close her eyes and smile and say, "It sounds wonderful!"

At other times she would have a spirited discussion about how to prepare a terrific ratatouille for the reception following the funeral. Sometimes Dorothy's mind would lose concentration and she would hallucinate for a few moments. Then she would suddenly look at me and say, "Where did I go just then? I don't think I was entirely rational. Poke me if I do that again."

The last time I went to see her, all her children were there. My wife, Wendy, came with me at her request. We had a simple service of Holy Communion at her bedside using bread and wine from her kitchen. Then we made a circle of hands around the bed and prayed together, each member of her family adding a few words of his or her own, thanking Dorothy for the joy of their life together and thanking God for (as one son said) "taking her on in the next." We all laughed at that. She wanted to sing something. We had a hard time deciding what hymn to sing because Dorothy kept changing her mind. Finally we sang "Amazing Grace" with a little bit of four-part harmony. Dorothy put her head back on her pillow, exhausted but happy. An hour later she died.

For Dorothy there was a tender longing for death, a supreme trust in God's loving care and an acceptance of herself as a valued and valuable person. Earlier I spoke about faith as having two sides: one side is our trust in God and in God's healing power, the other is our trust in ourselves as persons worthy of respect and love. Dorothy had both. For her, death was not a denial of life. Far from it. As she said, "It is God's way of healing me now; the only way I can get well is to die."

I tell you these stories, not to suggest that one is morally better than another, but simply to lay them side by side and to affirm that every death is the crossing of a threshold. At that moment God reaches out his hand to take hold of ours to take us with him on the next leg of our journey of life.

What about sudden death? The sudden, unexpected death of someone we love is an almost unbearable shock. But many people tell me that for themselves, that is the way they would prefer to die. In older times, the church assumed that everyone wanted time to prepare for death, and "The Great Litany" in the Episcopal Prayer Book contained the prayer, "Lord, Deliver us from sudden death."

No one has a desire to die prematurely, or to suffer a violent end. But the idea that one might go to sleep one night when all one's life's work is done and just not wake up seems to many the best way to go. I have always loved that prayer from the Prayer Book:

> O Lord, support us all the day long, until
> the shadows lengthen, and the evening
> comes, and the busy world is hushed, and
> the fever of life is over and our work is
> done; then in thy great mercy grant us a safe
> lodging, and a holy rest and peace at the
> last; through Jesus Christ, Our Lord.

Unfortunately, in this age of medical wonders and horrors, many of us will not die that way. The hospice movement has given us confidence that we can go through our final illness without severe pain and with great personal support, even if we are alone in the world. What we need most as we face our own dying is the confidence that there will be someone who will sit with us at least some of the time, and just be companionable, sometimes talking with us, sometimes sitting silently reading or knitting, doing little acts of kindness.; Someone who will respect our own way of dying and not feel the need to tell us how we ought to be doing it or what we ought to believe; someone who will keep a light hand on our worries and a cool hand on our forehead, not filling the air with chatter, but filling the room with quiet cheer. That is how hospice volunteers are trained. Because of their wonderful assistance, today no one need fear facing death alone.

As Christians we are sustained by the belief that we will awaken to a new life with a loving God. Then the divine love will shine upon us even more brightly than it does now. It will be like walking out of a dark room into the sunshine. St. Paul said, "Now we see as in a glass, darkly; then we shall see God face to face."

When I was a little boy I used to fall asleep on the couch in our living room. I would wake up in my own bed, and I knew how I got there; my father had carried me upstairs in his strong loving arms. Every now and then I would awake on the journey upstairs just enough to feel his whiskery kiss on my cheek. Even now I imagine that when I die it will be like that. And I even imagine that on that final passage, I will feel the brush of God's kiss on my cheek, and I will know that I have died, and that I am all right, and that all is well.

Let us pray:

God of Wonder...
Giver of Life...
Energize us...
so that...
Our faith may give us the vision and the mission;
Our hope may give us spirit and energy;
Our love may be grounded in the miracle of your love.
Sustain us in the pain of our losses.
Be with us as we continue our walk into the future with an open heart
So that we will discover a new future,
A new life,
Because we have become fertile again.
As Isaiah prayed...

See, I am doing something new...
Even now it comes to Light; can you not see it?
Let us go forth now in gentleness, peace and joy.
Through Jesus Christ, Our Lord.

Amen.

5

JOURNEY OUTWARD, JOURNEY INWARD

A Sermon on Prayer

I heard about a British sailor who scribbled the Lord's Prayer on a piece of cardboard and tacked it up over his bunk. Every night he would climb into his bunk, wave his hand toward the cardboard and say, "Lord, them's my sentiments."

If only prayer were that simple! I think everyone here tries seriously to pray in time of need. Isn't that why we are here, to try to forge a more intimate relationship with God and to build a faith that will sustain us in tough times? If we are a typical congregation, we will have a great variety of tales to tell about how we feel about our prayers: feelings of satisfaction or frustration, of comfort and healing or a sense of failure in our prayers. In my experience, most people feel some sense of shame about their prayers. They think that prayer should be natural and easy, and since they have difficulty with prayer there must be something basically wrong with them. How come, when they pray to God, it doesn't always help? Or it feels as though God isn't listening. One friend said to me, "I drag my body to church, but my soul seems to be back home with the unmade bed and the dirty dishes, and I don't know where God is."

Prayer, as I have come to understand it, is a gradual process of building a relationship with God, a progressive turning towards God over and over again in a thousand moments and ways until we reach the point where prayer isn't just something we do a couple of times a day, but a dimension of our whole life, of every thought and feeling.

The goal of prayer is not to find out who God is, though we do come to know God in the course of our praying, but to find out who *we* are. *God's* purpose for our prayers is that we come to see ourselves as the person he knows us to be, the person God loves, and so to heal the deep inner split between who we truly are and who in our worst moments we are afraid we are, or who the world keeps pushing us to be.

Prayer is a developing love affair with God, and like all love affairs it has its ups and downs. But because God does love us she enables us to see ourselves more clearly, more realistically and more compassionately. Because God loves us we can come to love ourselves in spite of all the stupid and selfish things we do. When we can love ourselves, then we can love others. Contrary to what we generally believe, I think it is an illusion to think that we can love others more than we love ourselves. I do not believe we can love others more than we are able finally to love ourselves. That is what Jesus meant when he commanded us to love our neighbor as ourselves. As we devalue ourselves, we inevitably will devalue others.

Prayer is a journey that goes in two directions: it goes outward towards the world that God loves, and inward to the soul that God loves. We can't have one without the other.

All Saints has long been known as a church that calls us to the outward journey. We cannot come here on a Sunday without hearing the trumpet awakening us from complacency, calling us urgently not to turn our eyes away from the world's wounds and sorrows. All Saints has always tried to translate its preached words into programs and institutions and ministries that bring hope to the larger community: Union Station, the AIDS Service Center, the Children's Center, the Office of Creative Connections, the Foothill Free Clinic, the Center to Reverse the Arms Race, the Skid Row ministries, and so many others. We have given these ministries freely as a gift to the community around us and have not tried to hold on to them. They are the evidence of our outward journey. We have taken our prayers out of our hearts and put them into our hands. As George Regas has often said to us, "Take your prayers out into the world and find God in the work."

But sometimes we have grown tired. The world's problems seem to grow bigger even as we engage them. We hear pleas for help from our congregation, help in forging a stronger relationship with the risen Jesus that will sustain us in doing love, pleas for help in renewing our flagging faith so that we can see the world's pain without turning our eyes away in sheer exhaustion or hopelessness at the immensity of the task. And so we know that we must support each other in the inward journey to meet God in the deep places of our souls, to feel God's touch on our aching hearts and to know God as the source of our strength.

The journey inward is the pathway to the heart, which has its own mysteries and reasons that Reason does not understand. Yet it is there that we see the tracings of God's finger in our lives. There are many roads, stages, and paths on the journey inward: prayer, meditation, Bible reading, psalms, music, and poetry. But in the end, we all make the inward journey in solitude and silence.

In some ways the inward journey is harder than the outward journey, because the world sees our outward journey and, if it doesn't punish us for it, it may cheer us on. But the inward journey goes against the grain of everything the world teaches us. We go alone, and we go in silence. Nothing in the world teaches us to value solitude or silence. On the contrary, the world insinuates that solitude and silence are signs of unpopularity, of failure, of death. So it shouldn't surprise us that the inward journey frightens us. Everything tells us it won't work. And when we do try it, we go deep inside and as likely as not we find no one is there: no God, no Jesus, not even any self—or so it seems—just emptiness and the dull pain of being all alone in a silent universe. Or so it seems. So we are likely to shun prayer and to feel ashamed at our spiritual barrenness.

That was my own personal experience. In the early years of my ministry I did all the things that my calling as a priest required of me: prayers every morning and evening right out of the Book of Common Prayer, bible reading, and retreats. I was dutiful, but I did not feel rewarded by much sense of God's companionship. So I kept busy with my parish work. That way I wouldn't have to face the uncertainties of my prayer life. In Peter DeVries' novel, *The Mackerel Plaza*, there is a priest of whom it is said that having lost his faith, he threw himself with redoubled energy into the work of his parish. Well, I hadn't lost my faith, but I worked longer and longer hours to rationalize to myself that I didn't have time for the inward journey.

The reality was that I was afraid—afraid that I would fail at prayer, and afraid that failing at prayer I might lose my faith. Then my priesthood would have become a charade. Better to keep busy and avoid the dark, dubious journey to the empty chambers of my soul. But not to pray was another kind of dilemma: what kind of a priest would I be if I didn't pray? So I binged on prayer. I would set myself rigorous spiritual disciplines and would lash myself to the oar once or twice a day and embark on my journey of prayer. This would go on for a while until something came up to interrupt my discipline. Then I would promise myself to return to my schedule. But days, sometimes weeks, even months would go by with no prayers, and I finally had to admit to myself that I didn't like praying.

I have come to believe that each person has to find his or her own prayer path. The inward journey takes different forms for different people. None of us can compare our prayers with any one else's. Each of us is unique, and everyone's prayers are unique. In my case, I finally found my inward journey in the most unexpected way. Some of you know this story. Fifteen years ago I was lying in a hospital bed after an operation that the doctor said revealed an inoperable cancer. It was late at night. I stared at the ceiling filled with fear and a sense of utter helplessness. I had given up trying to pray for myself. God was a million miles away. In the darkness I heard God speak to me, not words, just an idea that formed itself in my mind with absolute clarity. How did I know it was God? I cannot tell you. The heart has its own mysteries; I just knew. God simply said that I would be all right. I knew instinctively that did not mean that I would get well, but that it didn't matter. If I got well, I would be all right and if I died I would be all right because I belonged to God. Everything that I was, and everything that I ever would be in the future, was safe in God's hands. In that moment all my fear left me, and I closed my eyes and slept in peace.

From that moment on I have known that I am not alone. My life is caught up and held in God's love. I began to pray in a new way, not trying so hard to chase after God but to learn how to sit still and let God come to me as he had in the hospital room. I remembered the words of the Psalmist, "Be still and know that I am God." I decided to trust that. I am a very restless person, and it is a major achievement for me to sit still even for ten minutes. But I have come to love the stillness for itself, and for the delicious freedom it brings from the impulse to jump up and do something, for the freedom just to be me and to be with God.

In the stillness I discovered the miracle of my breathing. I never thought that breathing was such a big deal. But I came to believe that God was in the breathing; and I would concentrate on that intently, breathing in peace and love down into the tiniest cell in my body, breathing out fear. I could believe that God was in that breath. After all, isn't the Hebrew word for "spirit" (*ruach*) the same as the word for "breath"?

And I learned to quiet my mind. That was even harder, because my mind is an idea factory. (I shouldn't be surprised at that; that is what minds are for.) But the thoughts run pell-mell through my head. I had to learn to let thoughts slide by, or to dissolve like vapor, like sand castles washed away by the sea. In the stillness of my mind I am able to feel a glorious freedom from the tyranny of its ceaseless flood of thoughts. It takes practice, like my backhand, but it can be done, and it brings an exhilarating sense of control of my person.

Just this much enables me to open a great space in the hollow of my being where I can rest with God. I know that God is in that space, whether I feel her or not. It is holy ground, not because of anything I do but because of the peace that is there. I believe this is the core experience of prayer that both Christians and non-Christians have described for centuries. We can add to it in many ways, especially with scripture and with visualization of Jesus engaged in his ministry. But at the center is the stillness, like the axle point of a wheel around which rotate the activities of our lives.

The journey inward and the journey outward alternate. They tug at each other. Mother Theresa of Calcutta wrote that she could not do one without the other. The journey outward goes through the soul to the world, and the journey inward goes through God's suffering people to reach the soul.

This prayer is our pathway to a deeper sense of reality. Not only do we see ourselves more clearly but we see events and people with more clarity and compassion: the world's hunger, the painful plight of the boat people, the insanity of violence. We see the interconnectedness of all parts of life as we "put on" the mind of Christ, look through his eyes, feel with his heart and are sustained by his strength. We do not have the psychological strength to live his love without him. The collect for the nineteenth Sunday after Pentecost tells the truth: "O God—without you we are not able to please you..." Let us join hands then with one another on that journey of love.

> O God, forasmuch as without thee we are
> not able to please thee, mercifully grant that
> thy Holy Spirit may in all things direct and
> rule our hearts; through Jesus Christ Our
> Lord, who with thee and the same Spirit
> liveth and reigneth, one God, now and for
> ever.
>
> Amen.

6

FORGIVENESS:
THE HEALING OF THE HEART AND MIND

I. Deciding to Forgive

L et me begin with three situations that actually happened. I will come back to them later in these talks on forgiveness.

1. Mary's husband fell in love with her best friend, leading to a bitter divorce. Mary sustained a double betrayal and a triple loss: her husband, her best friend, and her dream of a happy marriage. Question: Should she forgive her husband and her friend? Why?

2. A middle-aged couple lost their daughter when she was murdered by three boys from the poor village in Africa where she had gone as a volunteer to help. Question: How could this couple forgive the boy who killed their daughter?

3. A sixty-year-old businessman was betrayed by his business partner, who stole all of his assets in the business and hid them in a Swiss bank account. He had to start all over at age sixty. Question: What justice would be served by forgiving his partner?

These are the kinds of questions that trouble us as we try to live our lives according to Christ's teaching about forgiveness.

Christianity is hard! All invitations to an easy Christianity should be avoided. They will lead to disillusionment.

Forgiveness is a prime example. It is at the heart of the Christian ethic. But it goes against our gut instincts, and to most of us it seems at times to be unrealistic, if not impossible. It is fairly simple to forgive small slights and unintentional injuries. But when someone betrays your trust, or steals your husband, or tells lies about you, or snubs you and doesn't care, your hurt is deep and your anger is great: you are not greatly moved to forgive that person—Christian ethic or no Christian ethic.

Some of what I am going to say in these talks can be found in Lewis Smedes' book, *Forgive and Forget*. It is a fine book, comprehensive and sensitive. But it has a provocatively misleading title. Forgiveness does not mean forgetting. In fact, true forgiveness *requires remembering* as clearly as possible. I think what the late Dr. Smedes meant by his book title is that true forgiveness can diminish the power of painful memories to the point where they do not torment us any more so that, while we don't exactly forget, at least we are not remembering all the time—and we are not full of chronic anger and resentment.

Chapter 6: Forgiveness

Why Forgive?

But why should we forgive someone who has done us harm, especially if it is deliberate or if the person has no regret? Isn't it more *just* to make him suffer the consequences of our anger and our contempt? Isn't our anger more *honest* than any contrived forgiveness offered at the behest of an idealistic ethic? These are not simple questions, because there is truth in all of them.

Why should we forgive? First, because God commands it. God did not say we should forgive if we want to, or if we find it reasonable. God made it a core condition of a God-centered life. Without forgiveness, God's creation would become corrupt and crash. It is a divine imperative. Jesus forgave his enemies from the cross. He was obedient to God's command: "Father, forgive them, for they know not what they do." But they *did* know what they were doing. Jesus meant that they did not understand the consequences of what they were doing. They only saw what was on the surface.

Jesus showed us the way. No torment we will go through could be more devastating than his. Of course, we can protest that he was the Son of God; we are ordinary garden-variety human beings and can't be expected to do what Jesus did. Wrong! It was Jesus' unique vocation to show us how to live the God-centered life.

Jesus told Peter that he was to forgive not seven times but "seventy times seven," which means there is no legal definition of forgiveness. It is a state of mind, a disposition of the heart. We have to keep on forgiving as long as we live. It is the only way to purge our souls of rage, resentment and the passion for revenge.

Forgiveness is embedded in the Lord's Prayer: "Forgive us our trespasses as we forgive those who trespass against us." God is saying to us: "You must forgive your neighbor as I forgive you." God might say further, "Look, Clarke, I know you through and through; nothing you do or think is hidden from me, including your basest thoughts and the sins you have hidden from others. But I do not turn my back on you. I stay close to you in love, not because your misdeeds don't matter to me. But if I do not, you will become so burdened by the weight of your misdeeds that you will become cynical and stop caring. You will become less of a human being than you were when you were born; I will cease to matter to you any more. Without my forgiveness you cannot be a whole person."

So we come to the second reason for forgiveness: it is not that we are doing a favor to some brute who offended us, but that there is no other way for us to be whole. Jesus taught centuries ago what psychologists have come to affirm only recently: that the healthiest resolution of past hurt includes an element of forgiveness. In therapy it is important for patients who have been abused to be able to focus their anger on those who have harmed them, so that feelings of rage can be resolved. But just focusing and expressing our anger does not set us free. We used to think that just expressing our anger would make it go away. But that's not true. Anger feeds on itself and becomes a habit. Our goal is to use our anger creatively, and to let go of our fantasies of helplessness and revenge that inevitably accompany unresolved anger.

Only true forgiveness will resolve deep anger. This requires inner conversion of the heart, and the willingness to look at the one who hurt us with new eyes, the eyes of

Christ. I believe forgiveness is a miracle, a miracle of love. To forgive is to rise above our gut feelings and to participate in a miracle, which God alone can make happen. *It is not something we will do naturally.* Someone once said that the longest journey we will ever make is the journey from the gut to the heart. We tend to believe that our guts always tell the truth, that our gut feelings are more trustworthy than our minds or our hearts, maybe even than God's truth. Not so! Gut feelings are emotionally conditioned and culturally defined. It is hard to let go of the visceral logic of hate and revenge. But only the converted heart can set us free from the endless torment of past hurt.

What Is Forgiveness?

What is forgiveness? Lew Smedes, with helpful simplicity, described forgiveness as a four-step process—three "H's" and a "C": we <u>H</u>urt, we <u>H</u>ate, we <u>H</u>eal and we <u>C</u>ome together, or we <u>C</u>onnect. So, what are the four steps of forgiveness?

1. Hurt

First we *hurt*. The crisis of forgiveness begins when we have been deeply hurt by something someone has done to us, something that affects us personally. But we need to *feel* the hurt. Often we deny the hurt because we do not want to believe that someone we trusted has in fact hurt us. Or we may push the hurt aside because we think that in some way we may deserve what happened. Forgiveness is irrelevant until we accept the fact that the injury is real and that it hurts like hell.

Let me tell you a story about myself. Many years ago I
was serving a church in the East. There was a segment of
the congregation that did not want me to talk about social
problems. They thought it was too "political." Their
vision of the parish was that it should be "picturesque, a
garden of peace in the midst of a troubled world." I
rather liked that idea, and it did have a beautiful garden,
but I wasn't content with palliative Christianity, soothing
people's hurts without asking why they were wounded. I
didn't think we should just rescue drowning people from
a river without going up stream to find out who is
pushing them in and trying to stop that. I could not
refrain from engaging issues of poverty and violence in
the community.

So I found myself in conflict with a segment of my
leadership. Without my knowledge, this group, led by a
man whom I considered to be a personal friend, started a
movement to get rid of me. Several people warned me
that this man was sabotaging me, but I could not believe
that he would do that to me, and I refused to take it
seriously. Even after it came out into the open, I did not
believe that he had betrayed me. Or, I should say, I didn't
want to <u>feel</u> it. It would have been too painful. I kept
thinking that there must be a good reason for whatever
he was doing, and that perhaps I deserved it.

When it finally hit me, I became enraged at him and cut
him out of my life. I did not want to see him or talk to
him. When I heard later that he had gone through some
major business and personal troubles, I was secretly
pleased. The point that I am making here is that there
wasn't any anger to deal with *until I felt the hurt*. Until then
there was no question of forgiveness. When the hurt

finally hit me, it took a long time for me to decide to forgive him.

Sometimes my patients tell me they were abused by a parent when they were children, but they are not aware of any sense of hurt. They don't want to believe that a parent who was supposed to love and nurture them would abuse them. In therapy we need slowly and carefully to elicit the buried anger so that the patients can deal with it consciously. Otherwise they will continue to act out of repressed anger and not realize it. The first step in forgiveness, then, is to acknowledge and experience the hurt.

2. Hate

Next we *hate* the one who hurt us. I want to recover the word "hate." It is a useful word and no other word expresses quite as well what we feel when we have been abused or betrayed. Most people say they don't hate anyone, especially Episcopalians who think it is bad form to hate. They say they just do not want anything to do with some people; they just want to cut them out of their lives. They do not care whether the person who hurt them lives or dies. That is a good definition of hate: when we hate, those who hurt us cease to be persons to us. We rule them out of the human race. We may say we do not wish them harm; but in fact if harm should happen to them, we wouldn't mind. I call that mixture of contempt and suppressed anger, "hate." The hate-crimes that are reported in the newspapers, such as painting swastikas on synagogues or gay bashing, can only happen if the perpetrators first reduce the victims in their minds to less than human status. The Nazis could not have succeeded in the annihilation of six million Jews if they had not first systematically portrayed the Jews as subhuman creatures to the German people.

Smedes discriminated between "passive hate" and "aggressive hate." Passive hate is the hate that doesn't wish your ex-husband harm but wants as little to do with him as possible; aggressive hate is the hate that wishes he would drop dead and his young new girl friend would get herpes. There is a spectrum of hate feelings. Hate is an *elemental inner violence* that dehumanizes the one who hurt you and sows the seeds of a life of resentment.

Some people say they hate the sin but love the sinner. I think that is an artful evasion designed to relieve one of the responsibility for facing one's buried rage. We do not like to think of ourselves as harboring hate; we think that by banishing the word we can banish the feeling. But we cannot separate the injury from the one who did it. We need to deal with both.

Hate is not the same as anger. Anger is a natural and inevitable emotion that we need to accept. It is a healthy emotion. When someone hurts us, our first reaction is anger. That is what we ought to feel. The sooner we recognize it and deal with it the less we will have to deal with hate later on when our anger goes underground. Hate is unhealthy and needs to be healed. Anger is creative energy and can motivate us to change things that are wrong. Hate doesn't want to change anything. It masquerades as anger but it becomes infatuated with itself and is never satisfied. It becomes a habit and corrupts our thinking and our feeling.

3. Heal

Then comes *healing*. With God's help, we heal ourselves. The healing act of forgiveness begins as a one-way street going from us towards the one who hurt us. It is a thrust of the heart. It is an act of the will. We make a decision to forgive. A theologian wrote,

> Forgiving is not for the weak-hearted or those who seek easy answers. Forgiving is indeed one of the truly courageous acts of the will. Forgiving is a power that challenges one to grow.

So, we make a start. In a moment of quiet reflection we look inside ourselves and we see the shadow that our hate has cast over our bruised hearts. And we say to ourselves, "Enough!"

- "It is *enough* that I have been hurt and treated unfairly."
- "I have let that hurt wound me over and over *enough* times."
- "I've let my anger feed on itself long *enough*."
- "Now I want to get rid of the shadow within me, the stain on my heart. I will no longer be held hostage to past wrongs."

In this moment we are only concerned with healing ourselves. What the one who hurt us thinks or feels about us is irrelevant. Our healing is our business. We take charge. We make the decision to put aside the past hurts and move on.

We do not wait until we feel like forgiving. If we wait for that we may wait forever. We make the decision as an act of the will. It is the first life-changing step on the journey we call forgiveness. The feelings will come later: feelings of relief, of calm, of hopefulness, of personal strength. The feelings follow the decision. I promise you, they will be worth the effort.

After we say "Enough!" to ourselves, we can call up a mental picture of the one who hurt us and say to him or her something like this: "I won't let you hurt me any more. You are a human being as I am, and a child of God. You have been weak and foolish and cruel. What you did to me was inexcusable. But my life belongs to me and I will not give it to you to hurt any more by keeping me stuck on hate. You take care of your life; I will take care of mine."

Then we cut that person loose and put him or her into God's hands forever. From that point on, every time the feeling of hurt and hate comes up—and it will come up again and again, often in the beginning, diminishing as time goes on—we return to this moment and repeat to ourselves, "Enough!" then put the feeling and thought aside again, turn the person over to God again, and allow ourselves to feel the *strength* that flows in behind our decision to be in charge of our own hearts. In our prayers we ask God to lift this painful burden from us. We cannot deal with it alone.

I said in the beginning that forgiveness is a one-way street. It may always be a one-way street for you. You may get nothing back from the one you are forgiving. But often, as your forgiveness works its miracle in your heart, you may find your relationship with the one who hurt you changing. Then the possibility arises of him or her responding, participating in some way in the process of forgiveness. Forgiveness then can become a two-way street, becoming richer and deeper for the sharing of the experience, even leading to reconciliation if that is what you want.

The young couple I mentioned in the beginning split up in an acrimonious divorce: the husband had gone off with Mary's best friend. Mary was so enraged that she refused to talk to her ex-husband and communicated with him only through her lawyer or curt written notes. About a year after the divorce, her teenage son and daughter sat their mother down and told her she had become bitter and angry and it was hard to be around her. They understood her anger at their father, but it had taken over their family and they were sick of it and wasn't there something she could do about it?

Mary was shocked at first. She had not realized how she had changed. After some painful introspection and further discussion with her children, she said "Enough!" and began the process of forgiveness. It was hard, because hate had become a habit. Slowly she made her way to the point where she could talk with him without sarcasm. After that for the first time they could have helpful discussions about co-parenting. She never excused what he had done or minimized the hurt she carried. But she let him back into the human race, saw him for what he was, and accepted the fact that he wanted to be a good father, as she wanted to be a good mother. To say that they were reconciled would be to say too much, but they connected, they came together in a way that allowed them to be effective, co-operating parents, to the great appreciation of their children. And her friends began to find in her again the warmth and humor they had known and loved before the divorce. The lifting of the burden of hate was the life-changing miracle that she had not even known she needed.

4. Coming Together

Coming together, or *connecting*: the fourth step in forgiveness varies greatly. For some there is a recovery of a broken friendship, for others, like the couple I just described, it may be just the ability to talk helpfully about important matters. Or in some cases it may be no more than simply thinking of the one who hurt you as an erring human being so that you connect with him or her as a person in your heart even if you never talk to each other. Some of my patients write letters to abusive parents who have died, expressing their feelings of anger and forgiveness, and then they read the letters to them by their grave.

You release the one who hurt you from the burden of your hate, even as you lift the oppressive weight from your own heart. And step by step, one day at a time, you let God help you carry the burden of forgiveness until it becomes as natural to you as breathing in and out.

The Church, the Body of Christ—the community of faith—lives by forgiveness or else it doesn't live at all. Sin is inevitable, and under its impact every church will either crack and break apart or, even worse, will stay together as an unhealthy cauldron of suppressed hate. Without forgiveness, the church can exist like an empty shell, but it cannot *live* as the body of Christ. Relationships within the church, like all human relationships, suffer from hurts, disappointments, failures, neglect, and even betrayals. Didn't the circle of Christ's apostles have to deal with all of these? It was only by Christ's forgiveness and the Holy Spirit that they rose above their anger and hurt and shame and became the Church. We know that, though often we do not act as though we know it.

We need to understand that anger is a *transitional* emotion. It tells us that something is wrong and needs to be changed. We do not want to end up in a state of anger but to move through it to serenity and peacefulness—to *shalom*. Forgiveness does not mean forgetting, or excusing or tolerating injury. It is the only way to do justice to our hurt and anger as we move towards the healing of our wounded hearts and minds, towards *shalom*.

II. Forgiving Those Who Are Hardest to Forgive

We have talked about the meaning of forgiveness, recognizing that it is among the easiest and the hardest of Christ's teachings:

- Easiest because we can forgive prematurely and superficially without really dealing with the hurt and anger we feel when we have been harmed or betrayed;
- Hardest because when we have been deeply hurt, at the gut level we want to strike back, to make the one who hurt us suffer as we have suffered, and to hold on to our anger as a matter of simple justice.

So how can we forgive when our feelings run so deep? I said that in true forgiveness we rise above our gut instincts by an act of the will to break the cycle of anger and the desire to hurt back which hold us hostage to past wrongs.

The new U.S. Ambassador to Vietnam, Pete Peterson, was an Air Force pilot who flew 67 missions over Vietnam before he was shot down; then he spent six and a half years in a Vietnam prisoner-of-war camp, a devastating experience. In the interview he said, "You have to make a decision to heal after an experience like that.... Your life then becomes so much more clear and unburdened—you are not always lamenting the past." That is up-to-date testimony about what I mean by forgiveness. We have to break the cycle of hate and vengeance and find a way to put our experience, however painful and unfair it may have been, at the service of some new good.

Some Things Forgiveness *Is Not*

There are some things that forgiveness is *not* but which get mistaken for forgiveness.

Forgetting

First, forgiveness is not *forgetting*. Real forgiveness requires remembering; in fact we cannot forgive unless we do remember. If we do not remember, forgiveness is irrelevant. Forgiveness is a decision that results in a miracle of healing of our hurt and anger in spite of remembering the painful things that were done to us. The memories will not completely go away. But their power to hurt us will diminish over time if we keep putting them aside without denying them. It may take a long time. We can't rush it. But we should not doubt that our forgiveness is real just because memories come back. Forgiveness is not forgetting.

Excusing

Second, forgiving is not *excusing*. It is not saying that the harm that was done to us didn't matter or that it couldn't be helped. It did matter. And it did not have to happen. True, it will matter less and less in terms of its impact on our present day lives as we forgive. But forgiveness includes holding people accountable for what they did even as we stop the cycle of retribution and anger. When my friend whose business partner stole his assets in their business decided to forgive him, it was not to excuse him and let him off the hook; it was to free himself from the unrelenting torment of his own rage. He did everything he could to hold his partner accountable for his theft. But he put his hatred for him aside and turned him over to God. Forgiveness is not excusing.

Tolerating

Third, forgiving is not *tolerating*. It is not accepting abuse as inevitable so that we just become numb to its effect. We do not want to develop a tolerance for abuse or betrayal or unfair treatment. When a neighborhood boy used to pick on my eight-year-old son, I confronted him. We had a serious talk, and I helped him to understand how his behavior was not only hurting my son, but that it was hurting himself by making him disliked on the block. He stopped his bullying and my son and I forgave him. But we did not tolerate his behavior. Forgiveness includes making every effort to stop abusive behavior, or to get away from it, and resolving not to tolerate that behavior in the future. Forgiveness is not tolerating.

What Forgiveness *Is*

If forgetting or excusing or tolerating are not what forgiveness is about, then what is it? Forgiving is deciding to take charge of our own hearts and the healing of its hurts and rage. It means confronting the one who hurt us, either in person or, if that's not possible, in our imagination, and saying to him or her something like this: "Enough! What you did to me did me great harm and I have been hurt and angry. You have been weak and foolish and cruel. But I will not let what you did continue to hurt me by keeping me stuck on hate. I am going to put the past behind me and put my anger aside and get on with my life." That is hard to do at first, but not as hard as you might think if you let God help you carry the burden of forgiveness.

Forgiving Monsters

But aren't there some people who do such terrible things that we cannot forgive them or we shouldn't forgive them? Shouldn't we keep the pressure of our anger on them for the rest of their lives? Or at least hold on to our anger as a reminder of how we were hurt?

There is a real life story that can help us understand how love transforms the most terrible of circumstances into faith and hope. Some of you know the story of Amy Biehl, but I will tell it to you briefly. Amy grew up in Southern California and while at college she became passionately committed to the anti-apartheid movement in South Africa. But she went further. A Fulbright Scholar, she went to live in Guguletho, one of the desolate black townships in South Africa, to help them in their struggle for equality. There she worked shoulder to shoulder with the poorest of the poor for political and economic betterment and freedom.

In 1993, near the end of her planned 10-month stay, she was murdered by three black youths who lived in the township. They stoned and stabbed her to death. At their trial, the youths could not explain why they did what they did. They sat there confused and disoriented. They had just struck out mindlessly at a white woman, a symbol of their oppression. They were sentenced to fifteen years in prison.

Amy's parents, Linda and Peter Biehl, were overcome with grief. Unable to understand how it could have happened that some young men would kill their daughter who had given her life to help them, they went to South Africa in search of answers. They went to Guguletho where Amy had lived and worked, and where the young men lived who had killed her. When they visited the mother of one of the boys and saw the squalid shack in which the family lived, when they saw the poverty in which all the people of the township lived, and when they experienced the oppression of the black people, they began to understand how rage and violence could fester there as the people faced the hopelessness of their lives. At that moment, Linda and Peter Biehl made a fateful decision: they would carry on their daughter's work. They would vindicate her so that neither her life nor her death would be wasted.

Linda and Peter Biehl came home to California and raised about half a million dollars in their daughter's memory. Throwing in their own life's savings, they went back to Guguletho. There they set up a program to train young men in trades of welding and brick-making. They set up after-school programs in music and art and mathematics and reading so that all the children could get some joy in life and could look forward to entering college after school.

The young men who killed their daughter sought amnesty under Bishop Tutu's Truth and Reconciliation Program. Amy's parents attended the hearings. They did not object, but supported the boys' petition, and the boys were released after serving three years. Amy's father said, "We were totally committed to the Truth and Reconciliation process. Hard as it was to see them go free, we had to accept the outcome for those boys as we would for any one who was granted amnesty for confessing their crimes."

The Biehls have continued to expand the programs they started, creating workshops and a bakery where young men and women can not only learn a trade but can get paid and build up savings. They said, "We go to South Africa so often now that we feel more at home there than we do here. When we are there we feel connected to life and healing and hope."

Linda was asked if she felt closure about Amy's death. She replied, "No, we don't seek for that. We just keep on moving in the work we do in her name and we believe that somehow, somewhere she is watching and cheering us on." Bishop Tutu said of them that they have turned the world upside down. Instead of asking for reparations for Amy's death, they are giving their lives to help those who killed her. He said, "It is an example of great humanity, of generosity, compassion, hospitality, caring. That is how love is ultimately more powerful than any other force."

This is more than just a charming story. It is a real-life parable. Linda and Peter did not go to South Africa to do good. They went in anger and grief. But they were overtaken by love. They were surprised by love. (I use the word "love" in its ethical sense, not its sentimental sense.) Something of Amy's devotion and dedication soaked into them when they weren't expecting it. Something of the desperate need of the people touched them. Something of the inevitability of the violence in the township jarred them. Something of the absolute necessity of a love that can overcome the hate penetrated their hearts and their minds. It had to be. There was nothing else they could do with their lives that made sense. In spite of their rage and their hurt, they had to go forward. They just couldn't go back

How Can We Forgive God?

And what about God? How can we forgive a God who allows such crimes, who would create a world in which such tragedy and suffering can happen? There is a part of us that is afraid to tell God what we really think of him. So we may just turn off to God, maybe keep going to church for some reason other than to worship God, and eventually just drop out. We say to ourselves, "If that's the best God can do, we can do without God." I was such a person.

I was raised an Episcopalian. I knew all the intellectual reasons why it is a good thing to believe in God, why it is at least possible that there is a God, even though there is no way of proving it. I was attracted to the mystery and beauty of religion and of churches. But the Second World War was devastating for me—the atrocities of the Nazis and of the Japanese, and sometimes even of our own troops, the calamitous bombings of innocent civilians in London and in German and Japanese cities, and the horrors of war in the jungles of Burma where I served. It became impossible for me to believe in a God who would create such a world, much less preside over it. So I left the faith of my childhood behind me along with other worn out toys.

On Christmas 1945, after the Burma campaign was over, I was in Kunming, China. I was so demoralized and so homesick that I decided to look for a church. I was directed down a maze of crooked city streets and suddenly by some miracle found myself standing in front of a little Episcopal church. It was Christmas morning, and the service had already begun. I slipped into a back pew. The service was in Chinese, which I did not understand. But I recognized the liturgy of the Eucharist. I knew exactly what was going on. I even recognized some of the hymns from my youth, and I hummed along. I sat in the back of the church, alone but surrounded by companions of the heart, and I cried and cried. The word "companion" means "to share the bread." At the Eucharist I shared the bread and was overcome by a sense of communion with these fellow worshippers, these strangers who, curiously, were friends. I felt connected to the transcendent God, the God of order and beauty and peace who had eluded me.

For the first time, I had the clear sense that God was not a myth. He was with me there in that little church. He was with this small congregation of Chinese who were still suffering through years of war. God had been with me through my months in the jungle and I did not realize it. For the first time I understood the meaning of the crucifixion; God was not sitting high on a heavenly throne watching Jesus die on Calvary. God was on that Cross. St. Paul said, "God was in Christ reconciling the world unto himself." Christians are the people of the crucified God!

Whatever problems we might have with God—and we have had plenty—He is with us, his children, in the tragedies and sufferings of our lives. He feels the horror of them as deeply as we do and yet is not destroyed by them. And so, as we hold onto him in faith, we are not destroyed either.

Why doesn't God stop the tragedies? I do not know. But I can appreciate that if God is love, then love is the most powerful creative force in the universe. Love cannot compel a responding love; such a response can only be freely given. That is not an explanation that completely satisfies us. But it helps us understand why God's power is self-limiting.

I came away from that Chinese church with these ideas ringing in my mind and lifting my heart. Did I forgive God then? No, but it was a beginning. I knew that for every one who died strengthened by God's presence there were hundreds who died in lonely fear. Still, I came more and more to understand the power of faith. If we live only under the shadow of fear and anger, we cannot escape a deadly spiritual paralysis. It is easy to think of faith as a soft option, to be enjoyed if you have it, to be regretted if you have not. But in fact faith demands what love demands and what forgiveness demands: an act of the will, a firm and forceful hold upon reality. It is a positive and glorious and flaming thing, which often glows more splendid in the darkness.

Forgiving Ourselves

Finally, let me say that sometimes the hardest person to forgive is one's self. Our sense of failure; our hurtful anger towards others, especially those we love; our secret suspicion that we have not been honest; our sins, negligences and offenses against the innocent of the world—these self-accusations, usually exaggerated and distorted, build up in us and we push them down into our unconscious minds where they become a source of projection and obstacles to our forgiving others. Then we put on others the repressed anger we feel for ourselves.

Forgiveness of others must go hand-in-hand with forgiveness of ourselves; otherwise it will never happen. We will love others only as much as we love ourselves, not one bit more. Here again we need the bridge between God and ourselves. We are his children. He does not forget our sins, or excuse them or tolerate them. But he wants the humanity, the precious gift he gave us at our birth, to grow in us. That can happen only by the power of the "Love that will not let us go."

God Was in Christ, Reconciling the World to Himself

If we think that love is just a sentimental idea compared to real worldly powers—physical, military, financial—we can look at the Biehls and see for ourselves how their love is working a transformation that no other power on earth could effect. That is the meaning of the cross. If we open ourselves to the proposition that it was the incarnate God who hung on the Cross for our transformation, we begin to enter close to the mystery of God's being.

The Easter resurrection dawns for us upon the seemingly irreconcilable dilemma of the crucified God. But the Resurrection is more than just eternal life winning out over death. It is God winning out over all the human rage and violence that drove him out of the world: the greed, the betrayal, and the lovelessness that drives God's weakest and poorest children to the margins of society. It is God's transformation of the human tragedy.

When we go to the Eucharist, let the sorrow stir our hearts. Without dying there cannot be any resurrection. Without wounding, there cannot be any healing. Although for many of us our lives are reasonably comfortable, still there are many of us who bear in our hearts sorrows so deep that only the agony of Christ can reach the deep place of our pain. Some of us have lost children or life partners; some of us have been abandoned by a spouse or lost a home. Some are caring for children with birth defects or for parents with dementia. Some of our hearts have been broken by the plight of the homeless or by the victims of war.

On the cross God himself bears all pain. We recognize that God cannot prevent the pain in the world. He cannot take back the radical freedom he has given us. He has no choice but to come himself and take upon himself the pain that results from the freedom he gave—then to lead us to higher ground, to hope and faith and promise as he did the Biehls. What they did is of God. God is there. We can see him and name him. Their love has taken them and everyone in South Africa above and beyond ordinary human experience.

So, when you go to the Sunday Eucharists you join yourself to the Biehls, to Amy, to the wounded God and to the risen Christ. Let yourselves be carried beyond anything that the human will or imagination can achieve on its own without the power God's forgiveness and love.

7

THE SPIRITUAL QUEST AND PSYCHOTHERAPY

Where the Faith Journey and Psychotherapy Join Hands In the Healing of the Mind

Many people do not avail themselves of psychotherapy, even though it may be the best available source of health at a particular time in their lives. They reject it because there is a stigma attached to psychotherapy. Church people especially tend to think that psychotherapy is antagonistic to religious faith, that if we had enough faith, we wouldn't need therapy. I believe it is urgent to address this problem.

I have thought a lot about the various ways to address this subject, and have made a choice that may surprise you. I think it might be more helpful to you to hear something about my own personal experience. I have lived on the frontier between faith and psychology, the borderline between religious practice and the practice of psychotherapy, for forty years as a priest and as a licensed psychotherapist. I have grown in my understanding of how spirituality and psychology join hands in the healing of the mind. Telling my own story might be more lively and useful for you than just a lecture on psychology and spirituality. So here goes.

When I had been in the ministry for ten years, I was pastor of an impoverished, struggling, inner-city church in New York. Discouraged, weary, but always hopeful, I was a faithful, hard-working priest who believed that with God all things are possible.

One night I was having dinner with a dear friend, a psychiatrist named Frederic Flach, and after dinner he took me aside. He said he wanted to see me in his office the next day. "Why?" I asked. "Because I think you are depressed," he said. I objected vigorously. I was a little offended. I didn't feel depressed; I was working hard. Why on earth did he think I was depressed?

He replied that over the course of the dinner and conversation that night, I had told him that I was waking up at four o'clock in the morning and worrying about my work, that I was having trouble concentrating and making decisions, I wasn't getting much pleasure out of life, and my self esteem was at a low ebb. "These are clinical signs of depression," he said, "and I can help you." Fred's analysis of my emotional state offended my idealized sense of myself as a saintly priest on the way to martyrdom. I wasn't aware I had said all that, but a quick mental review of my dinner table conversation confirmed that I had indeed revealed all those things about myself. So I went to see him.

Quickly my idealized self crumbled into its opposite, abject self-deprecation. I saw myself as a religious fraud who had been caught in my deception. Of course at that time I had never heard of the tendency of the distressed mind, especially the depressed mind, to alternate between idealizing one's self and deprecating one's self without being able to find a stable and credible middle ground.

Over the course of the next fifteen weeks, Fred helped me to see more clearly and realistically some of my patterns of thinking and behaving. I learned that:

1. I was taking care of everyone except myself, without adequate time for rest and recreation.

2. I thought that to take time to do nice things for myself was self-indulgent.

3. I thought that if anything went wrong, somebody was to blame; so I was constantly in a state of harsh judgment, either of myself or of somebody else, instead of accepting as inevitable the foibles and the failures of ordinary beings, including myself.

4. I had a driving need to prove myself to be a competent person, and I had a relentless hunger for approval. Even though other people were not actually that critical of me, I imagined that other people were constantly judging me.

5. I maintained a steady but superficial demeanor of niceness and pleasantness to everyone, and covered up my anxiety and my anger. I thought that was what priests were supposed to do.

These were just a few of the persistent patterns of thinking that added up to an unrealistic view of myself. I was neither the saint that I aspired to be, nor was I the fake and failure that I feared I was. I was just a garden-variety priest doing a better than average job in a difficult situation.

Where did these ideas come from? My friend Fred, the psychiatrist, helped me to trace these attitudes to their source, to early experiences and relationships with important people in my life when I made incorrect and distorted judgments about myself and had never corrected them.

As a result of my fifteen sessions with Fred, I experienced a great sense of relief, a recovered energy, and an end to my four o'clock awakenings. He said there was more I could do for myself through further therapy, but that this was a good start, and there was also medication if my improvement and my functioning didn't hold. I didn't go back to see him at that time, but in the forty years since, I have sought therapy whenever I found myself getting bogged down and anxious, getting overly hard on myself or handling relationships poorly. Therapy has always been for me a resource that I could reach out for. I came to see therapy as an avenue of God's healing for me.

I asked myself, "Why didn't prayer solve these problems? Why didn't God do for me what the psychiatrist did? Why wasn't faith enough?" I have always believed that God does not necessarily intervene *physically* in my life to prevent accidents or illness, but I have always assumed that God was always engaged with me spiritually, that is, on the *inside*, presumably correcting my moods, my feelings, attitudes, perceptions. I do not have a definitive answer to these questions, but I do have some answers that have been helpful to me. For example:

1. God did answer my prayers. God said, "Go see Fred. He has some skills you are not likely to find at the church, in the ordinary day-to-day church experience. Fred is part of my healing team."

2. Much of what I learned from Fred I already knew about myself, or at least suspected, but I would not accept it. I was in denial. I was resisting truths that I already had an intuition about. It took a therapist to get me to believe what God had been trying to tell me about myself for years.

3. At the center of the therapy experience was a genuine relationship with a caring person, a therapist whom I could trust and who would not judge me. He could help me examine my assumptions and see my life more realistically. Isn't that exactly the kind of relationship the Bible calls a loving one? Isn't a loving relationship always God's chosen instrument for the healing of the soul?

Sometimes, for all of us, God seems elusive and out of our reach. The very concreteness, the flesh-and-bloodedness, the immediacy of the therapeutic relationship is what made it work for me. The relationship between the therapist and me, empathic and warmly human, gave me the courage to believe in myself and to try myself out in new and healthier ways. He was a channel for God's healing love to me, even though, in the course of our therapy, he never mentioned God by name.

This example of my own therapy is an ordinary one. I was not paralyzed by anxiety or acting out in grossly dysfunctional ways, although I could have been. I was not dealing with profound melancholy or mania or personality disorder. But I was not functioning well, either. There were strains in my marriage that I didn't understand, and my parish was not getting the best there was of me. I was on the edge of anger a lot of the time. I am pretty sure, when I look back on that time, that if Fred had not gotten hold of me when he did, that I would have blown it someday, and maybe I would have eventually quit my job or damaged my career irreparably.

As we know only too well, most people resist the idea of psychotherapy. Why?

- Some say, "I should be able to handle this myself." They think that therapy is a sign of weakness or of failure.

- Some people do not trust therapists. Everybody has a pet horror story about a "shrink."

- Many feel that there is a stigma attached to being in psychotherapy, so that others will think less of them if they find out that they are seeing a therapist. Do you remember the Thomas Eagleton situation? Thomas Eagleton was George McGovern's running mate for Vice President of the United States in the 1970's. He was a very able public servant, and he was a fine candidate for Vice President. But some journalist found out that at one point Senator Eagleton had received treatment for depression. He was forced to resign from the campaign because of the furor stirred up, especially by his political opponents. The concern about stigma is real.

- And, as I have said, church people have a particular type of resistance to therapy, because they think that God alone should be enough, that prayer should heal everything, and that psychotherapy is a sign of inadequate faith.

After my own experience with therapy, I saw it as my duty to my congregation to build a bridge between the practice of religion and psychotherapy, so that people would no longer see them as "either/or," but see them as two avenues of God's healing that serve the same goals: the definition and nurturing of the "self."

The faith journey and psychotherapy are parallel paths that find their common ground in the care of the psyche. "*Psyche*," as you may know, is the Greek word for "spirit." In psychiatry, we call it the "self." What is the self? It is our mind, our will, our conscience, and our emotions. It includes both the conscious and the unconscious aspects of the self. Therapy and spirituality both concern themselves with the best functioning of the self.

In *The New York Times* there was a harrowing story of a lovely seventeen-year-old high school boy in a small town in Maine who committed suicide. No one could figure out why. He was an excellent and popular student, a fine athlete, a seemingly well-adjusted if reticent and quiet kid. One night he walked out into the woods behind his house and hung himself. I am sure that that youngster was wrestling with some deep emotional pain, and that he believed that there was no one he could talk to who would understand and be able to help him. I am sure that the prevailing attitude in that town was that only wimps and weirdoes go to counselors and shrinks. The local churches probably also conveyed the idea (as they so often do) that if you just had enough faith and pray hard enough, all problems would be solved by God. This boy had been faithful at church, but it was not helping.

No child or adult should feel ashamed to seek help, nor harshly criticize him or herself for lack of faith. No one should live tormented by fear. Spirituality, in contrast to psychotherapy, is the practice of reaching out, through prayer and worship and scripture and the fellowship of the church, to a God who loves us and wants us to be our best selves. But pain—both physical and emotional—can block out the sense of God's presence in our lives. Psychological distress can so darken our moods and distort our image of ourselves and our sense of God that it can become all but impossible to pray. In those times, therapy may be God's chosen avenue of healing. That may include medication, and it may include hospitalization.

I do not know why faith sometimes is not always enough. But I do know that some traumas of the mind require special treatment, just as some traumas in the body require special treatment. Also I know that God has given us other tools, other insights, other ways of understanding and engaging "the self" that are only hinted at in the Bible. These are being constantly researched and spelled out in the world of psychiatry.

Religious faith believes that there is meaning in life beyond the self. Faith goes beyond the self to engage God, the Divine Other, the Higher Power, the Risen Christ—whatever you want to call the One who, I believe, is the governing spirit of the universe, who is the source of our hope and our peace. To engage God is at the same time to engage and affirm our *self* with ever-increasing realism, because, I believe, God wants us to know him (or her) in order that God can show us to ourselves. Thomas Merton wrote,

> The secret of my identity is hidden in the
> love and mercy of God... I discover myself
> in discovering God. If I find Him I will find
> myself; if I find my true self, I will find
> God.

Some religious people may object to that. They will say, "Aren't we supposed to deny ourselves?" The religious idea of "selflessness," a very profound and important idea, does not mean the obliteration of the self, or the masking of the self, or the deprecation of the self. Jesus said, "Thou shalt love thy neighbor *as thy self*," not "better than thyself;" not "Love thy neighbor and hate thy self." Love your neighbor *as* yourself. That is a moral imperative.

Selflessness means to cherish the self, which we then freely offer to God in love. We offer the self that we are coming to understand, along with our love, to God as a self-offering. The miracle of God is that when we offer ourselves to God in love, we discover we do not lose ourselves but, as Merton said, we discover ourselves in new and truer ways.

Religious faith tells us that there are some things that are not just good, they are *sacred*. For example, the loving care of children, the protection of the innocent, the preservation of the environment, and respect for human life. These are not just good social policies; I believe they are sacred trusts and moral imperatives. Spirituality is the quest for the *source* of those imperatives whom we call "God," and the honoring of that source in worship.

I do not mean to suggest that, just because psychotherapy is secular, that it is mechanistic or that it lacks moral perspective. I do not mean to suggest that, to a psychologist, the most noble thoughts of man are only chemical secretions. Therapists find human relationships as mysterious, as awesome, as wonderful, as any priest does, and they find the psyche equally precious. But the therapist works on the human side of the divide between the human and the divine. Generally speaking, they are neutral with respect to religion.

I had a patient once who was not a member of my church. She was a young woman who as a child had been sexually molested by her father. She was furious at him, but she also loved him. She was torn by ambivalent feelings of rage and affection. She was also tormented by feelings of guilt that she might, in some way that she couldn't grasp, be responsible for what happened to her. She was also angry at her mother, who she believed must have known about the incest, or at least suspected it, and did nothing to stop it. The mother maintained that she never knew about it.

The goal of our therapy was to work through the problems caused by the incest that were showing up in my patient's own marriage. There were sexual and intimacy problems in the marriage, and a pattern of angry outbursts at her husband.

It was not the goal of therapy to deal with her religious life, though that was important to her and she did talk about it. She told me that she attended church quite regularly, but that she had never been able quite to trust a God who was seen as a divine parent. And she had never been able to trust herself as a spiritual person because of her guilt.

In the course of her therapy she came to see that the incest was in no way her fault. Her father was totally responsible; he was the adult. He had done a wicked thing; he had broken a sacred trust. My patient decided to reconcile with her parents. Not everybody who has been sexually assaulted would make that choice, but she did. Once she understood that forgiveness does not mean forgetting or even excusing what her father had done, she decided to forgive her father. She found the courage to confront the father with her anger. She was also able to talk to her mother in a new way without having to know whether her mother knew about the incest. So she was able to establish a new kind of relationship with her parents a few years before they died, which was what she wanted even though there had been abuse and neglect.

The problems in her own marriage diminished as she gained insight and a sense of control over her own life. These were her goals in going to therapy. But in addition she found that she could pray again, and that she could receive the love of God for herself and the strength to forgive.

I tell you this story because it illustrates what I am trying to say. The young woman had seemed to be living her life on two tracks, one spiritual and the other psychological. Ostensibly there was no crossover between the two: no psychotherapy in the church, and very little discussion of religion in the therapy. But in fact *the psychotherapy and the spiritual practice served each other.* God gave his healing spirit through both channels to bring about in my patient a more mature sense of herself and also a more mature sense of God, and the dichotomy between them disappeared in the healing of the self.

A therapist has written, "Psychotherapy helps us to know ourselves better, to relate to others with integrity, and to live in the world with less fear, more wisdom and increasing pleasure. But therapy stops short at the world of the spirit." That is a good statement, but I would change that last sentence. I believe that we are all spiritual creatures, whether we are religious or not; our human spirit and our self are the same thing. Therapy limits its work to the self and its human dimensions. However, when the self thrusts *beyond* itself and reaches out to a higher power, to God, for meaning and self definition, for a love that is greater than the sum of all of our loves, then in that moment we cross a boundary. And once past that boundary, we tread into the world of faith where God is the source of all healing, where our peace and our hope surpass all human understanding.

8

A CHURCH FOR ATHEISTS

I am teasing you with the title of the sermon. I do not mean that All Saints Church is a place where God is not believed and taught. Quite the contrary. At the center of our life and worship is a traditional understanding of the classical Christian faith. But we have a low threshold at our front door so that a person who doesn't believe in God, or doesn't know if he does or not, can come here hoping to find God and not be looked down on by the members of this church. This is a church where an atheist can come in out of the cold and explore the possibility of faith.

If you are such a person this morning, a spiritual orphan searching for faith, this sermon is especially for you. I want you to know that there is a place here for you. There are corners in this church where you can hide if you want to and just watch what's going on, and there are groups and programs you can participate in without anyone asking you what you believe. We are glad you are here, and we hope you will join us on our journey of faith.

Everyone here is at a different place on that journey of faith. Some of us are just beginning our quest for God; others have been on the road for many years. But we are all together helping each other make our way into the heart of a mystery, a mystery that we will never completely understand, a mystery which is greater and more wonderful than all our explanations. That mystery is the love of God.

I want to make just two points in this sermon:

1. Atheists are welcome here because their skepticism deserves our respect.

2. Atheists are welcome because most of us here have experienced times of at least temporary atheism when, in our struggle with faith, God seems to disappear.

First of all, to any atheists, church drop-outs and spiritual wanderers who have come to this service, I want to assure you of our respect for you. I can understand why so many people find the idea of joining a church infinitely resistible. Religion has been the cause of so much intolerance, suffering, and persecution throughout history that many understandably think it better to stay away from it.

Early in the war in Bosnia, I saw a heart-rending documentary on TV. A Serbian Orthodox priest was interviewed about the war. He was wearing the military uniform of the Serbian army with chaplain's crosses on his lapels. He said that he was in favor of the war because the

Serbs had ancient grievances against the Bosnians and this might be their last chance to settle old scores. I couldn't believe my ears. Settle old scores! Somebody should have told that priest that Christianity is not about settling old scores! The religion of Jesus Christ is about forgiving and making all things new. It is about putting old antagonisms behind us, about breaking down the walls of hostility that separate us. St. Paul said that love keeps no score of wrongs. And Jesus, hanging on the cross, cried out, "Father, forgive them, for they know not what they do." That is the way Jesus settled scores with his persecutors.

The Serbian Orthodox priest then was shown anointing Serbian soldiers for battle, making the sign of the cross on their foreheads with oil. We know—the world knows—that many of those soldiers would kill innocent civilians, rape Muslim women, and drive elderly Bosnians from their homes. I know that there are many Serbs who have disassociated themselves from this terrible war, that there may be some of Serbian extraction in this congregation this morning who are horrified at what happened. But surely anyone watching that program would be forgiven for not wanting to be part of such a church. A simple sense of justice and compassion would turn him away.

And as for believing in a God who defends the innocent, the world has not been the same since the Holocaust. Where was God when six million Jews went to the gas ovens? In Kurt Vonnegut's novel, *Slaughterhouse Five*, a Jewish woman who has survived the horrors of a death camp shares with her friends her bitterness and her feelings of betrayal. She had been taught since childhood about a God who loved her and would protect her. She raises her glass in mock tribute, "Here's to God Almighty, the laziest man in town!" It is a scathing indictment of God. We shiver when we hear it. But we can understand how she feels, and we must respect her anger.

If the church is going to win the respect of the world, we must be willing to embrace those who have been hurt by the church, or who have not been able to reconcile the idea of God with the gross injustices they see in the world. We must warmly accept the spiritually wounded who "do justice and love mercy" but cannot yet acknowledge Christ. One time the disciples came running to Jesus complaining that some people were casting out demons but not doing it in Jesus' name. They asked him, "Should we stop them?" Jesus replied, "Do not stop them. Those who are not against me are for me." Jesus welcomes all who do good whether they recognize him or not. Whether they wear a cross or not, if they act and think in a spirit of love, they are his friends.

Alcoholics Anonymous is based upon the belief that there is a God who acts in our lives to enable us to overcome the compulsion to drink alcohol. They call God their Higher Power, so that anyone who has a big problem with God will not be discouraged from seeking the help of their fellowship. Tolerance is the pathway to their Higher Power. A member of this church who is in AA said to me, "It is a good thing they didn't put 'God' in front of me when I first came to AA. I would never have gone any further. I was so angry at God that I just wiped him out of my belief system. But slowly my Higher Power took on the characteristics of the God of our faith, so that finally I could embrace God again and return to my church. I am so grateful for their openness to accept me at the beginning without judging me."

Here at All Saints we try to express that openness with the Rector's weekly invitation to Holy Communion:

> Whoever you are, wherever you are on your journey of faith, you are welcome here at the Lord's Table. Come and receive this bread and wine made holy. It is God's free gift of new life for you.

There are some who think it is wrong to invite people to Holy Communion unless they are baptized. We have a different idea. We offer the gracious hospitality of the Lord's Table first; then we invite them to baptism when they have come to trust us. Like the father in the parable of the Prodigal Son who rushes out across the desert to embrace his erring son who has come home and spreads before him a welcoming feast, God, who is Father of the Eucharistic feast, reaches out to every searching son and daughter and embraces them in his church and welcomes them to his table.

Most of our newcomers at All Saints tell us that it was that invitation more than any other single thing that made them want to join our church:

> Whoever you are,
>
> If you want to be a peacemaker;
> If you feel a deep compassion for the
> homeless and the helpless,
> and want to do something for them;
> If you just want to find some peace for your soul;
> If you want to find healing for a broken heart;
> If you yearn for a life that has more meaning
> than just a bleak journey between two oblivions...

Then come and live for a while with us.

We want all those things too. And let us introduce you to Jesus who may have eluded you thus far. He is the source of inexplicable support even in the darkest of times.

The second thing I would say to any atheist or spiritual seeker who may have found her way into our midst this morning is that I believe most of us who call ourselves Christians have our times of doubt and even loss of faith that can be for us like bone-dry stretches of atheism on our otherwise joyful pilgrimage of faith. Even Jesus cried out in despair on the cross to a God who seemed to have abandoned him: "My God, why have you forsaken me?"

We build our lives on our beliefs. But sometimes in critical moments in our lives we feel the termites of doubt gnawing at the foundations of our faith. It may be a time of great pain, either physical or spiritual, and the pain seems to block out God as totally as an overcast sky blocks out the sun. Or we may be so anxious that we find it impossible to pray. Or we may be kneeling in church saying those prayers that have comforted us for years and suddenly realize we are not sure we believe what we are saying, that we do not *feel* God's presence. Then we are assailed by the fear that maybe our house of faith is really just a house of cards. I have been in those places myself. I know how devastating those dark nights of the soul can be, especially for a priest who is supposed to be an unwavering source of buoyant faith.

One of my theological heroes is C. S. Lewis. In the years of my own undergraduate agnosticism, it was his brilliant explanations of Christianity that led me back to the faith of my childhood. Countless Christians owe their faith to his writing. But when his wife, Joy, whom he married late in his life, died of cancer, even this great Christian found himself in the grip of despair. He kept a journal of the terrible days of her dying. He wrote:

> ...where is God? ...turn to him (when you are happy) with gratitude and praise, you will be—or so it feels—welcomed with open arms. But go to him when your need is desperate, when all other help is vain, and what do you find? A door slammed in your face, a sound of bolting and double bolting on the inside. After that, silence. You may as well turn away. The longer you wait, the more emphatic the silence will become.

Slowly, painfully Lewis made his way through the haunted woods of his despair to a renewed sense of God. But his faith was never again so tidy, never as glossy as it had been before. I think all real faith that has been tested in the battles of life is a scarred and bruised faith, bearing the marks of our struggle to hold on to an invisible God.

I doubt that there are many happy atheists. That is, I am not sure there are many people who enjoy their belief that God doesn't exist. I think mostly there are agnostics, people who don't know what to believe, or how to find God, or whether they even want to find God in view of so much seeming evidence of Divine neglect. All of us here are reaching for something that is beyond our grasp, reaching for something above us so that we won't sink to something beneath us. In the eyes of some that makes us hypocrites, because we profess more than we fully understand and commit ourselves to more than we can accomplish. I saw a man standing on the sidewalk in front of my church in New York one Sunday morning. He was looking rather glum, so I asked, "Why don't you come inside? We're going to have a worship service in a few minutes." "Not on your life," he replied. "I wouldn't be caught dead in there with all those hypocrites." I said, "Well, come on in anyway. There's always room for one more."

God is always beyond our grasp. But we are never beyond God's grasp. William Sloane Coffin, the minister of New York's Riverside Church, went to see his friend Norman Thomas, the great Socialist leader, when he was dying. Coffin asked him if he was feeling at peace with God. "Oh, Bill," Thomas sighed, "I'm not sure I even believe in God." Coffin replied, "That's all right, Norman. God believes in you, so I promise you, whatever happens you are going to be all right." The old man's eyes filled with tears. He took hold of Coffin's hand and said, "I wish somebody had told me that years ago."

Atheists, agnostics, wounded souls, spiritual wanderers: whoever you are, by whatever name you call yourselves, you are welcome here and we are glad you came. Join us in a humble pilgrimage with God; a God who we believe will not be an offense to your conscience. Bring with you your anger and your skepticism and your rigorous honesty. God will make good use of them; He will put them at the service of love. Sometimes we feel that we are like the blind leading the blind. But at least we are not the bland leading the bland. God respects your indignation and will use it in the battle for justice, that very same moral indignation that led you to reject God in the first place.

We do not claim to have all the truth there is about God, but we believe we are on a journey towards the truth, and Jesus, who lived the truth, is our companion. Come and join us on the way. Because, as one theologian said, "HELL is arriving at the truth too late."

9

CHILDREN OF THE ATOMIC BOMB

A Sermon Preached on the 50th Anniversary of the Bombing of Hiroshima and Nagasaki

On August 6th, 1945, as a 19-year-old veteran of the war in Burma, I was driving a U.S. Army truck full of radio gear over the famed Burma Road into Western China. Like my two brothers who were in the Philippines, I was on my way to join the vast build-up for the invasion of the Japanese homeland which we all knew was coming.

One of my older brothers was a Marine and the other was a paratroop doctor. I thought they would probably be among the first to land on the beaches of Japan. I, with my radio, would not be far behind. Suffice it to say, the three Oler sons, an entire generation of Olers, was poised for what everyone knew would be the most costly operation in terms of American lives ever to be mounted.

The Americans had already sustained staggering losses in the Pacific war. But the greatest battle of all lay ahead of us.

The news of the atom bomb attacks on Hiroshima and Nagasaki, and then the news of the Japanese surrender, came through to me on the Burma Road. I can remember as though it were yesterday the overwhelming feeling of relief, of deliverance.

My parents kept a neat file of all my letters. The other day, curious as to what I wrote on that occasion, I reread those letters. They were bursting with thanksgiving that there would be no invasion, and that the terrible war was finally over. "O, my God," I wrote to my parents, "we will be together again; we will be coming home."

When General MacArthur was signing the surrender documents on the deck of the battleship Missouri, the voice of a crewman who had forgotten to switch off his microphone was heard over the sound system; "Brother, I hope those are my discharge papers!" That was all any of us thought about. It never occurred to me to ask if the bombings were a good thing.

As time passed, and I became aware of the magnitude of the devastation wrought by the bombs, I felt a dreadful ambivalence: those bombs which I believed saved my life, and my brothers' lives, turned out to be the most terrible device ever unleashed upon mankind. Today is the 50th anniversary of that bombing. Some of us who were actually engaged in the bitter battle against the Japanese forces remember the exultation we felt when the victory came. Today we are called by God to remember the price of that victory, and the kind of weapons and tactics that both we and our enemies resorted to in that war.

⁂

It is always the Christian community's duty to remember. It is central to our worship, and essential to our hope. When he established the Eucharist, Christ said, "Do this in remembrance of me." "Do not forget my humiliation and suffering on the cross; do not forget the lies, the betrayal, the cruelty, the full range of human sins that caused my crucifixion. Do not forget the power of God that raised me from the dead and gave me the victory over the cross." That victory was not one of human powerfulness, but of God's commitment to life, of God's refusal to turn the world over to the forces of evil. On the mount of the Transfiguration, God's voice thundered out of heaven to the three vacillating, bewildered disciples, "This is my beloved Son, listen to him!" The further we get away in years from what happened fifty years ago, the more the dreadfulness of it fades, and the more we lose clarity about what really happened to those cities and their people, the less we are moved by God's command. By remembering, we listen.

God is in the remembering. In a few days we will remember and celebrate the end of the war. I hope we will celebrate that right gloriously. It was the end of an incredibly painful and costly conflict. But I hope we will be thoughtful in our celebration. The Japanese people are now our friends. They were taught by fanatical leaders who led them through horrible military adventures. That is the remembering that the Japanese must do. They need to remember the rape of Nanking, Pearl Harbor, the

Bataan death march, and the infamous prisoner of war camps if their suffering is to give way to hope. Yesterday, at the peace observance in Hiroshima, the mayor of that city said to the world, "We want to apologize for the unbearable suffering that Japanese colonial domination and war inflicted on so many."

We need to remember not only the terrible effects of the atomic bombs but the fire bombing which largely destroyed almost all of Japan's sixty-six biggest cities. General Thomas Power, the commander of the U.S. bomber forces, estimated that the firebombing of Japan's cities resulted in half a million civilian deaths. Forty percent of all urban housing in the entire nation was destroyed and 20 million people were left homeless. He described the firebombing of Tokyo in March 1945 as "the greatest single disaster incurred by any enemy in military history. It was greater than the combined damage of Hiroshima and Nagasaki. There were more casualties than any other military action in the history of the world." We need to remember, not to stir up our guilt, but so that we will not minimize, we will not be tempted to glamorize what we as a nation believed was necessary to fight and win that war. Without remembering there cannot be any hope.

❧

Today commemorates the dawn of the nuclear age. Those were the only two atomic weapons ever exploded against an enemy, so they present us with the only specific record of what an atomic attack is like. Yet most of us do not remember: we were not there, or, like me, if we were around at the time, we didn't pay attention; or we have numbed our consciousness because the suffering of

Hiroshima and Nagasaki is too hard to look at. We have to remember what most Americans have never really known. That is the important task of today, if we are to let the agony of those cities lead us to hope and a renewed commitment to life.

In 1962, Robert Jay Lifton, a research psychiatrist at Yale, went to Hiroshima to study the psychological effects upon the survivors. He found them, in spite of their stoicism and enormous spirit of recovery, still traumatized seventeen years later. The best way to describe his findings is to see the Hiroshima experience as taking place in four stages.

The first stage was the initial immersion of the people in the sea of dead and dying after the bomb fell. He called it, "the permanent encounter with death." Survivors recalled not only feeling that they themselves would soon die, but that the whole world was dying. Mutilation and destruction was everywhere. They believed the world was ending. One man said, "The feeling I had was that everyone was dead. The whole city was destroyed. I thought all my family must be dead. It doesn't matter if I die.... This was the end of Hiroshima, of Japan, of humankind." They referred to themselves as walking ghosts, or as one man said, "I was not really alive."

The second stage was what Lifton called "invisible contamination." Within hours or days or weeks after the bomb fell, people began to experience grotesque symptoms: severe diarrhea and weakness, ulceration of the mouth and gums with bleeding, bleeding from all the body openings, high fever, very low white cell count, usually following a downward course until death. Most people didn't know what it was; they spoke of a mysterious "poison." It evoked a widespread terror that soon everyone in Hiroshima would be dead. None would escape the poison. Even the unborn babies were affected, many being born with misshapen heads and severe mental retardation. Then the rumor began to circulate that trees, grass and flowers would never again grow in Hiroshima. From then on Hiroshima would not be able to sustain any kind of life. It was total death.

The third stage occurred years after the bomb fell with the emergence of various forms of leukemia, the fatal malignancy which became know as the "A-bomb disease." Over decades there was an increase in various forms of cancer—thyroid cancer, breast cancer, stomach cancer, bone-marrow cancer, lung cancer. And there was a pervasive anxiety. Even 17 years later, one doctor said, "The fear never completely goes away. Take my own case. If I am shaving in the morning and I should happen to cut myself very slightly, I dab the blood with a piece of paper—then when I notice that it has stopped flowing, I think to myself, 'I guess I am still all right.'" The people retained the profound fear that at any moment the A-bomb disease might break out in them, and, worse than that, they might transmit this deadly taint to future generations. To this day, nobody knows for certain the extent of the permanent genetic damage. As one woman said who was pregnant at the time and who survived the blast, "When will the silent bomb within us explode?"

The fourth stage was the persistent identification with the dead, as though the dead were the legitimate ones, and those who survived had somehow borrowed a life they did not deserve. In many cases it caused the survivors to feel they were living "as if dead." They became in their own eyes a death-tainted group, as though they were in some vague way carriers of a fearsome destiny. Many of them carried the keloids on their faces and bodies, the thick scars of the burning, visible reminders, they thought, of their collective shame. They did not speak of their experience because they were often discriminated against; they were poor bets for employment because they might develop the disease, and their children would have difficulty finding marriage partners. At a deep level many retained a sense of guilt that they remained alive while others died, and for not having been able to do more to save others. What could they do about the keloids on their souls?

This was the experience of two small Japanese cities. You and I hear it now as if for the first time, and we say, "We did not mean it to be that way. We just wanted to kill the soldiers and stop the war. We didn't know."

Now we know! And, strange to say, their story is their gift to us. The memory of their suffering is their gift, not to stir up our guilt but to remind us of the terrible cost of war and the threat nuclear weapons pose to the survival of the human race. But their gift to us is greater than that: they have given us their recovery, their courage, their incredible good will instead of hatred, their commitment to peace instead of revenge. On this day of all days, they do not point the finger at us, but they reach out to us to join them in their determination to rid the world of atomic weapons and to forge an alliance with us because, like them, we know the dreadful truth.

❦

I have said that God is in the remembering. That is not the whole truth. Yes, the remembering is essential to hope. But remembering by itself can make us cynics. Seeing again the savagery of the past can destroy our trust in human beings, including our trust in ourselves. We need to see through the human tragedy and beyond it to the vision of life on this planet as God envisioned it when he created it. The people of Hiroshima and Nagasaki have embodied that vision. That is their greatest gift of all. God is in their healing, and in their ability to rise above national and religious differences to reach out in the name of peace. I must add that I believe God was also in the just and compassionate American occupation after the war.

The Japanese Nobel Prize-winning author, Kenzaburo Oe, writing recently in *The New York Times*, reminded us that among those who died in Nagasaki were more than 8,000 Christians. The rebuilding of their city and of their lives has been an interreligious and international effort. He wrote, "With the rebuilding the surviving atomic victims are trying to move their recovery into something larger so that they may pass their faith on to those who are to come in the next century."

Today we face not only the threat of a war between nuclear powers but a nuclear accident, or a terrorist attack. America must take the lead in renouncing atomic weapons and weapons testing. That is not a simple thing to accomplish. We cannot dis-invent the bomb. But the enormous creativity and intense effort that went into the making of the bomb we must now turn to the un-making of the nuclear threat. We are currently engaged with Russia in the reduction of our nuclear arsenals. We must do everything in our power to maintain and enlarge that effort through treaties and increasingly effective verification. We must continually inform our leaders of our absolute commitment to that goal.

Einstein said, "We are like infants playing with dynamite ...and thus we drift towards unparalleled catastrophe." The use, or the threat of use, or even the mere possession of nuclear weapons presupposes leaders of superhuman wisdom and self-control. Democracy accepts that our leaders are fallible human beings who all too often, like the people who elect them, "know not what they do." But they can be held to account, they can have second thoughts, and they can put mistakes to right. No one can put to right mass death and the contamination of the earth—the inevitable result of a nuclear war.

What we do here together as church people at All Saints will not be insignificant. We need to keep the pressure on our leaders and our politicians to work tirelessly for realistic and effective control of nuclear weapons with a passionate goal of abolition. Our leaders need to know that we have not gone to sleep. The urgency is even greater now as more countries are developing the nuclear capability. In the 1980s, *TIME* magazine had a cover article attributing the awakening of the American people to the nuclear danger to the grass roots efforts of groups like ours (church groups, community groups, protests of all kinds) forcing the issue on the public conscience.

William Sloane Coffin, one of the most effective voices for nuclear abolition, said recently:

> "Once again it is up to us who are furthest from the seats of power and therefore nearer to the

heart of things. So let us not wear an air of futility like a crown of thorns. Let us not hesitate to lead. Only after we have proposed, educated, advocated and lobbied will our politicians consent.... There are still about twenty thousand atomic weapons around. This is the equivalent of seven hundred and fifty thousand Hiroshima-size bombs, about one point two tons of TNT for every human being on the earth.... I am wary...of ineffectual purity. But if we do not bury nuclear war in the sands of history, the human race is likely to go the way of the dinosaurs which became extinct through too much armor and too little brains."

If God is in the remembering, God is even more important in the making of the peace. That was the meaning of Jesus' life, the Prince of Peace; of his death and resurrection; of God's command at the Transfiguration: "This is my Son, my Chosen One; listen to Him. Listen to Him! You have my precious world in your hands."

The Japanese people once lost their way in war. We must not lose our way in peace. In our national proclivity for optimism and happy endings, we do not like to look into the heart of darkness, but on this day we must and we do. We do not dare to succumb to collective denial. We must re-awaken to the dreadful power of annihilation that we possess in our nuclear weapons. There are some clouds that do not have a silver lining.

Today we let the people of Hiroshima and Nagasaki, the dead and the living, be our teachers, so their suffering will not have been in vain. With the help of Almighty God, the author of all hope, we let them lead us now. For we, too, are children of the atomic bomb.

10

IT IS TOWARD EVENING,
THE DAY IS FAR SPENT

Across the street from my church in New York City there was a row of old apartments called tenements. When I first arrived as the new minister there, I called on the residents of those apartments looking for lost sheep. There were quite a few! One was an eighty-six-year-old woman named Helen. She had lived on that block her entire life. She had sat on the curb as a little girl and watched the church being built, and had been a regular parishioner all her life.

But when I discovered her, she hadn't been to church for a few years. Three flights of stairs were hard for old legs. Most of her friends had died or moved away, and it was painful for her to be reminded of so many lost friends. So when the rector she had known for so long died, she couldn't bring herself to adjust to the new one. She wasn't lonely at home; she was lonelier at the church where no one noticed her anymore.

I finally persuaded her to start attending a weekday luncheon which we began for a group of elderly women who sat on the benches in the garden in front of the church. That led to her becoming a "grandmother" to one of our Sunday School classes where the children excitedly showed her their crayon drawings and climbed into her ample lap. Finally she came back to worship with new friends.

The message the church gave to Helen was similar to the one the disciples had given to Jesus on the road to Emmaus: "Stay with us. For it is toward evening and the day is now far spent. Stay with us. We have a place for you. You belong here with us. Don't stay alone. It is getting late."

Three years to the day after she returned to church, Helen died. She hadn't been afraid of dying, but she hadn't wanted a memorial service. She was afraid no one would come. "I would shiver with embarrassment in my grave if you held a service for me and no one came," she said. But her memorial service was attended by a hundred people who had come to know her, including her luncheon companions, several teen-agers who used to help her down the stairs on Sunday mornings, three sixth-grade Sunday School classes who, over the years, had had the task of walking her across the street to church, a group of mothers whose toddlers had sat on her lap in Sunday School, and assorted parishioners who had escorted her to doctor's appointments. In those three years, Helen had found a new family in the Lord's house.

"Stay with us. For it is towards evening and the day is now far spent." The disciples had extended that welcome to the stranger who they met on the road to Emmaus. "Stay with us. Don't go on alone. It's late." And when they broke the bread at the table, they recognized Jesus.

Jesus often said, "If you show kindness to any other person, you are showing it to me. If you make a place for any one who is old, or a child, or who is a wandering soul, you are making a place for me. If you give so much as a cup of water to a thirsty person, you have done it to me." I don't know whether anyone who came to love Helen discerned in her wrinkled face the face of Jesus. But he was there, hidden, unnoticed, unnamed. He would have said it didn't matter. The important thing was that you cared. You took the trouble. That is all Jesus would ask.

As our parishioners canvassed the buildings around the church, we found many elderly people who were isolated in their apartments, virtual prisoners of their frailties. They couldn't get to the markets or the clinics or the doctors' offices. I heard of one woman who died of starvation in her apartment because she couldn't get out to buy food. And then there was a woman I used to visit who wouldn't go to the doctor because it was too hard and she didn't want to be any trouble to any one to take her. I found her very ill one day and insisted on taking her to the emergency room at a city hospital. I couldn't stay with her, so I told the nurse about her and said I would be back in a couple of hours. When I got back to the hospital, I found that she had died in the waiting room. These experiences led me to initiate a program we called "Search and Care," to find homebound persons and arrange for volunteers to shop for them and escort them to the clinics and sit with them until they were seen. Over the years the program has flourished. They take care of hundreds of homebound persons every month so they won't have to go into nursing homes until it is necessary.

I think for all of us the time is late. We are already far into the night of neglect for our most vulnerable citizens. The value of human life in our society seems to grow cheaper by the day, especially for the homeless and chronically ill. The night is far spent. Jesus walks the streets unnoticed. He is often old and wrinkled and lame, and no one says "Stay with us." Against this dark backdrop, it is easy to overlook the elderly. They are so old, we think. They are not useful.

In our inner cities, gangs of hoodlums sometimes prey upon the old because they are defenseless and they don't matter. A few blocks from my church a gang of twelve-year-old boys set fire to a sleeping derelict and burned him to death. They said they didn't think of him as a person. "He was just an old bum," they said.

At our church we used to say there was no such thing as an "old person," there were just persons of special value because they had been with us for a long time. Personhood has no age. It is as real in a ninety year old as it is in a child. If you want to know whether any society has the spiritual power to endure, notice how the people treat their elderly. If they are preoccupied with youth and physical strength, that society will die. Indeed it is dead already.

There are many myths about the elderly which we can dispel:

> · Most elderly people are not unhappy;

- Most elderly people are not lonely;
- Only a small percentage of persons over 65 live in some kind of institution;
- Most elderly people continue to be as creative and interested in the world around them as when they were younger.

The theologian Henri Nouwen wrote:

> Aging is the turning of the wheel, the gradual fulfillment of the life cycle. Aging does not need to be hidden or denied, but can be understood, affirmed and experienced as a process of growth by which the mystery of life is revealed to us.

To those here this morning for whom — at least in terms of years or physical strength — it is still early in the day, I make this request: there are some persons among us who need your freshness, your vigor, your good legs, your good eye-sight, especially your loving concern. Can you give an hour or two a month to be with them, to discover them, to cherish them?

Please don't feel guilty if you have to say, "I'm sorry; not just now." There may be other persons who need you right now, or perhaps the person who needs you at this moment is yourself, the "you" that is inside that may be overburdened and exhausted. That person also needs to spend some quiet time with Jesus. But if you can help, speak to one of us following the service.

Whatever our world's night may bring tomorrow, whatever new holocausts or wastelands we may bring upon ourselves in the future, there is only one thing that matters: *caring*. The eyes of the caring heart can see in the dark; they notice the worth of those who are becoming invisible and cherish those who, as we say, have been with us for a long time. To those who need our youthfulness let us say, "Stay with us. It is towards evening. The day is far spent. Don't go on alone. You belong with us. We have a place here for you. Your wisdom and your story are our treasures." And if someone should reply, "Do not trouble yourself for me," we will answer, "It is no trouble. And even if it were, what trouble would we rather have?"

11

THE FAITH OF A
REVERENT CHRISTIAN AGNOSTIC

It is reported that a man once approached an English bishop and asked him anxiously, "Your Grace, is it possible to be saved outside the Church of England?" The bishop replied, "I suppose that is possible, but no gentleman would avail himself of it." I want to reassure you that it doesn't matter if you are a gentleman (or gentlewoman), you are safe! Your salvation is assured, because you are under the care of a loving God. How do I know? Let me try to explain.

I have come to the point in my journey of faith where I call myself a Christian agnostic. That does not mean that I do not believe in God. That would be atheism. Atheists are people who have given up looking for God, or who think that "God" was a bad idea in the first place.

Agnostics are those who accept that God cannot be known with intellectual certainty, but believe in Him anyway. Christian agnostics are those who say, "The big question is, 'How can I give my heart to Jesus without stumbling over the doctrines and traditions of the Church?'" There is for me, as for many, a knowledge of the *heart*. It is not certainty, but a conviction that arises from experience. The word "confidence" comes closer to expressing my knowledge of God: a knowing of my heart and mind that I cannot prove, but which is the foundation of my life. Is that superstition? Or is it an opening to mystery and grace?

All little children are agnostics; they believe in God, perhaps because their mommies told them He is real, though they would certainly be grateful if God would show up now and then so they could see him. One time when my children were little, we were at the dinner table and I admonished my son, Kim, not to pick his food up off the floor to eat it because it might have germs. My six-year-old Kim replied, "Germs and Jesus; that's all I ever hear around this house, and I have never seen either one." Agnosticism is not easy. We yearn for certainty, but we have to live by the untidy and inexplicable miracle of love.

The great American jurist Learned Hand, in an address in Central Park, New York, in 1944, gave magnificent expression to the American idea of liberty for which our people were engaged in fighting World War II. He said:

> Liberty lies in the hearts of men and women; when it dies, there is no Constitution, no law, no court can save it... What is this spirit of liberty? ...I cannot define it; I can only tell you my own faith.

> The spirit of liberty is the spirit *which is not
> too sure that it is right* (emphasis supplied).
> The spirit of liberty is the spirit which seeks
> to understand the minds of other men and
> women; the spirit of liberty is the spirit
> which weighs their interests alongside its
> own without bias; the spirit of liberty
> remembers that not even a sparrow falls to
> earth unheeded. The spirit of liberty is the
> spirit of Him who, nearly two thousand
> years ago, taught humanity that lesson it has
> never learned, but has never quite forgotten
> – that there may be a kingdom where the
> least shall be heard and considered side by
> side with the greatest.

That is the faith of an agnostic: one for whom liberty is
not a dogma or a document, but a wisdom of the heart
that speaks for itself. Though he is *not too sure that he is
right,* it claims his total loyalty. He will defend not only his
own rights but also the rights of others, the rights of the
least along side of the rights of the greatest. So it is with
the Christian agnostic, who *is not too sure that he is right,* but
lives his life as though he *were*—as a servant of the One
who, two thousand years ago, lived and died for the least
and the poorest and the powerless of the earth; the One in
whom the Spirit of the Universe that we call God
expressed his will for all people. (I say "his," but you
know that I mean "hers" as well. God is not masculine;
every creature, male or female, has been made in the
image of God.)

I "know" that there is a God, a governing Spirit at the
center of all life, and I "know" that Jesus lived as perfectly

as any man ever has the purposes of God. I "know" this, even though I cannot prove it, and in spite of much seeming evidence to the contrary. I "know" because no other life, no other death, has so grasped my heart and made sense out of my life and given me hope. I have experienced Christ not as an idea, but as a presence. Frederick Buechner, a Presbyterian pastor, wrote:

> All-wise. All-powerful. All-loving. All-knowing. We bore to death both God and ourselves with our chatter. God cannot be expressed, but only experienced. In the last analysis, you cannot pontificate but can only point. A Christian is one who points at Christ and says, "I can't prove a thing, but there's something about his eyes and his voice. There's something about the way he carries his head, his hands. The way he carries his cross—the way he carries me."

It has been my own experience that at the darkest times in my life when I have had to give up any pretense of being the master of my own fate, when I have let down the barriers of my soul and set aside the stern scrutiny of my intellect, and opened myself to the possibility of God's love, I have felt God's peace as an inexplicable mercy. In those moments I have been like the Prodigal Son in the Gospel story, all full of shame and fear, returning from a far country and seeing his father rushing across the sands to embrace him—an inexplicable mercy, a gift of reunion and hope, a promise of home at last. In the words of the Rev. William Sloane Coffin, "'God is love' is not a truth we can master, it is only one to which we can surrender."

However, faith is not just an inner, private experience. It must be expressed in the commitments we make to each other and to the society in which we live—commitments to peacemaking, to justice for the least as well as the greatest, to a compassionate society. Love is not just a feeling; it is the choices we make. As Rabbi Leonard Beerman has said, "We have to take it out of our heart and put it into our hands."

Jesus said:

> I was hungry, and you gave me food;
> I was thirsty, and you gave me drink;
> I was a stranger, and you welcomed me;
> I was naked, and you clothed me;
> I was sick, and you cared for me;
> In prison, and you visited me....
> Inasmuch as you have done these things to the least of my brothers and sisters, you have done them to me.

Christian agnostics hear that as a call from God to follow Jesus. As people of integrity and generosity and largeness of soul, they cannot wait until they figure out what the church means by the virgin birth or the resurrection of the body or demons or eternal damnation. As Thoreau once said, "One world at a time!" Jesus welcomes the Christian agnostic as he did the thief on the cross: "Today you will be with me in paradise."

George Regas—and now Ed Bacon—built All Saints Church on the premise that if you come here to worship you won't have to leave your brains on the coat rack at the door. God gave us a mind to use. He said, "Come, let us reason together." He gives us the right, indeed he gives us the duty, to be skeptics, not to surrender our minds to any religious authority or to any worldly authority; to question; to sort things out; to reach an understanding of what is true and just and lovely and genuine; to unpack, one by one, the scientific verities; to probe life's mysteries without giving up our sense of wonder.

So our church welcomes the unbelievers, the spiritual orphans, the questioners and the skeptics, the atheists who are not so sure about their atheism, the agnostics who want to believe in a Higher Power but are not ready to believe all the creeds and dogmas. Our invitation on Sunday morning is as generous as God himself: "Whoever you are, wherever you are on your journey of faith, whatever you may call yourself: Welcome! Come into the center of our life. Open your mind and your heart to a God who has been waiting for you. There is a place at his table for you." We are all spiritual wanderers who have committed ourselves to a God who does not quell all our doubts.

The psychiatrist Rollo May wrote, "Commitment is healthiest where it is not without doubt, but in spite of doubt." Our doubts are painful, but at least they keep our faith fresh! Without doubt our faith becomes stale.

We don't scorn our traditions and liturgy and doctrine here at All Saints. They keep us connected to our origins, to former generations of faithful believers and worshippers; they have taught us about God and Jesus, and they give coherence to our faith community and beauty to our worship. But they are not a closed system of belief. They need continually to be challenged, reformed, and opened up to new understandings and new expressions of God's truth. We Christian agnostics would say, with Bill Coffin, "Sometimes we need not only to recover our traditions but to recover from them."

Many of us Christian Agnostics make our way through and around Christian traditions and dogmas so that we can find enduring value in some of them and, as C.S. Lewis said, put the rest of them in a box marked, "Awaiting further light! " For me, the Virgin Birth is an example. It seems to have had little importance to the early church. It is only mentioned in two of the gospels, and not at all in St. Paul. I find it irrelevant to my devotion to Christ, and in many ways dangerous to the social welfare of women. For me, it awaits further light.

Dorothy Day, one of my spiritual heroes, the founder of the Catholic Worker Movement, established houses of hospitality for the unemployed and the poorest of the poor in cities throughout this country during the early part of the Twentieth Century. She found her way from atheism to the Roman Catholic faith. She gave her life without reservation to Jesus and to the homeless and the poorest of the poor, as Jesus did. Through the objectivity and tangibility of the sacrament of the Eucharist, she found the church a steadying influence for her idealism and her commitment to Jesus. Without deciphering what the church meant by calling Jesus "the Son of God," she was grateful for the assurance that the love Jesus lived was universal and grounded in eternity. She never for an instant let a dogma get between her and whatever was best for her beloved poor.

At All Saints we are not making God up as we go along. At the center of our life together is a deep well of faith that love is the central, creative, life-giving power of the universe; that love is reasonable and demonstrable even if it is beyond our power to prove; that the source of all love is the One we call God; that the exemplar of love is Jesus, though He is not the only one through whom God has revealed Himself. We believe that religion is but a garment of love, not the love itself, and like any garment, sometimes we grow out of it, it needs to be let out, it needs to be mended. We do not judge people by their garments, but by how love is shown forth in their lives.

At the center of our life is the Bible. We do not take it literally; we take it seriously. We do not deify the Bible. We recognize its inconsistencies and contradictions, because those who wrote the Bible were fallible human beings like ourselves. But in their own time they were men of God. And when we read in the Bible about Christ empowering the weak, scorning the powerful, healing the wounded and judging their tormentors, we know we are seeing God at work, and we know that God is Christ-like. Jesus crossed every boundary: boundaries of class, of nationality, of tradition. In every person he found the dignity of a child of God. The Bible tells that story.

The trouble with fundamentalisms and dogmas of all kinds is that too often they require us to settle for a faith that is too rigid to grow, that is not open to new vistas of truth, that will not allow new dimensions of God that they have not dreamt of. A faith that will not grow is a faith that has congealed. It is dangerous. So our faith is in a God we have not nailed down—who will not let us nail Him down, a God who has left the final knowing to our hearts. As Pascal said, "The heart has reasons that reason does not know."

Everyone here knows how dangerous, because of religious fanaticism, these times are. We may well be facing a war of civilizations. No matter how in such a tragic confrontation we may be driven to defend ourselves, ultimately the only way to defend our civilization will be to live out God's eternal realities of justice, peace, community, reconciliation, compassion, and love. These realities, as Judge Learned Hand said, lie in our hearts. But they exist in the world only to the extent that we choose them and live them—and, like Jesus, die for them.

I do not think of Jesus as a religious leader. I do not think Jesus had any interest in that, except as religion may distort God's truth. He did not come into the world to found a new religion called "Christianity," but to reawaken the Jews to God's demands for justice and compassion. He was God's moral will made visible, an exemplar of His love, and is therefore God's and our gift to the world. He had a unique and special role in God's revelation. But Jesus is not the only one in whom God reveals Himself. E. Stanley Jones was a great Christian missionary to India. He once said of Mahatma Gandhi: "Gandhi has taught me more of the spirit of Christ than perhaps any man in the East or West." There are many avenues of divine truth in the world's spiritual traditions.

Vividly I remember sitting in my foxhole in the Burmese jungle in WWII, my radio by my side, the enemy somewhere in the surrounding darkness. I looked up at the brilliant stars and the moon above me, and thought that people in each country of the world would look up as the world turned to see the very same stars and the very same moon. And I thought, if to each of us it were given to see the face of God, perhaps in time we could see each other as children of God, equally precious, equally beloved. We would then know that God possesses the secret of our common humanity and, regardless of our religion, we would look for that secret together.

How our minds yearn for certainty! But I believe there is none to be had, so I call myself a reverent agnostic. As valuable as tradition and logic may be, neither is greater than the wisdom of the heart.

Albert Schweitzer was one of the most accomplished and devout Christian men of the twentieth century—a great physician, a great theologian and a great musician. He yearned for the certainty that would banish his doubts and prove the validity of his faith, so he dedicated his towering intellect to writing a book entitled *The Quest for the Historical Jesus*. He failed in his quest to find certainty. But, undeterred, and inspired by Jesus' parable of the rich man and Lazarus, he founded a hospital in the jungle village of Lambarene in the Belgian Congo, and dedicated his life to caring for the most neglected of God's children. Schweitzer concluded his book with these words:

> He comes to us as one unknown, nameless; just as in an ancient time, by the lakeside, he came to those men who knew him not. He speaks the same word to us: "Follow me!" He places us at the *tasks* that we must fulfill in our time. To those who obey him, wise or simple, he will reveal himself in the labors, conflicts, and miseries they will experience in communion with him. As an ineffable mystery, they shall come inwardly to know who he is.

❧

"When the darkness appears
And the night draws near,
And the day is past and gone:
At the river I stand,
Guide my feet, hold my hand:
Take my hand, Precious Lord,
Lead me on."

— Thomas A. Dorsey
Precious Lord, Take My Hand

❧

ENDNOTES

Opening Quote:
Page 9, *The Reality of the Spiritual World* by Thomas R. Kelly.
Published in The Pendle Hill Reader, Copyright 1950, page 13.

Chapter 2: God Is in the Darkness:
Page 18, paragraph 1: "O Come, O Come Emmanuel" is Hymn 56 in the
Episcopal Church's 1982 *Hymnal*. The words were combined from various
antiphons by an unknown author, possibly in the 12th Century, as the hymn
"Veni, veni Emanuel." It was translated from Latin to English by John M.
Neale and published in *Mediaeval Hymns* in 1851. The music to "Veni
Emmanuel," is from a 15th Century processional of French Franciscan
nuns (the setting for the funeral hymn *Libera me*); arranged by Thomas
Helmore in the *Hymnal Noted*, Part II (London: 1856).

Page 20, paragraph 3: The movie *Shadowlands* (1993), was written by William
Nicholson and was produced and directed by Richard Attenborough. It
starred Anthony Hopkins as C.S. Lewis and Debra Winger as Joy Gresham.
The movie was adapted by William Nicholson from his own play of the
same name, which was loosely fashioned around biographical facts about
Gresham and Lewis. The film's production notes quote Mr. Nicholson as
saying, "I have used parts of their story, not used other parts and imagined
the rest," adding "no one knows exactly how and why they fell in love." For
a plot synopsis and review, go to the AllMovie.com Website,

http://www.allmovie.com/cg/avg.dll?p=avg&sql=1:131133

Page 23, paragraph 1: The third line of this verse from *O Come, O Come
Emmanuel* differs from the text at Cyber Hymnal's Website. Other variants
of the text also exist. John M. Neale's original translation from the Latin
began, "Draw nigh, draw nigh, Emmanuel."

Page 24, paragraph 2: Helmut Gollwitzer, ed., *Dying We Live: The Final
Messages and Records of the Resistance* (London: Fontana Books, 1958)

Chapter 3: The Healing Path
Page 29, paragraph 3: "I thank whatever gods may be" is from "Invictus,"
by William Ernest Henley (1875), a poem that originated several well-
known phrases. For more information than you might want about this
poem, see the *Wikipedia the Free Encyclopedia* entry at

http://en.wikipedia.org/wiki/Invictus.

Page 32, paragraph 3: Helmut Gollwitzer, *Dying We Live* (see above)

Chapter 4: Loving, Losing & Letting Go
Part I: Love and Mourning

Page 38, paragraph 0: C. S. Lewis, *A Grief Observed* (New York: HarperSanFrancisco, 2001) paperback 112 pages (originally published in 1961)

Page 38, paragraph 1: Judith Viorst, *Necessary Losses: The Loves, Illusions, Dependencies, and Impossible Expectations That All of Us Have to Give Up in Order to Grow* (New York: Free Press; 1998) paperback, 448 pages (originally published in 1986)

Page 38, paragraph 3: Samuel Clemens, *The Autobiography of Mark Twain*, quoted in Viorst, p. 238

Page 39, paragraph 1: Helen Hayes, *My Life in Three Acts* (New York: Harcourt, 1990) 266 pages

Page 41, paragraph 5: Lewis, *A Grief Observed*, p. 56

Page 42, paragraph 1: Tony Talbot, *A Book about My Mother* (New York: Farrar Straus & Giroux; 1980) 180 pages

Page 44, paragraph 1: Viorst, p. 278

Page 46, paragraph 1: William Shakespeare, *Macbeth*, Act 4, scene 3

Page 46, paragraph 4: Lewis, *A Grief Observed*, p. 6

Page 47, paragraph 2: 1 Thessalonians 5:17

Page 48, paragraph 1: Isaiah 43:19

Part II: Growing a New Self

Page 50, paragraph 2: Judith Viorst, "How Did I Get to Be Forty and Other Atrocities," quoted in Viorst, p. 266

Page 50, paragraph 3: Randall Jarrell, "Next Day," quoted in Judith Viorst, p. 299

Page 51, paragraph 4: Frederic F. Flach, *The Secret Strength of Depression* (New York: Lippincott, 1974) 288 pages

Page 60, paragraph 3: Isaiah 43:19

Part III: "As Dying and Behold, We Live!"

Page 61, subtitle: 2 Corinthians 6:9

Page 63, paragraph 3: Woody Allen, actor, director and screenwriter, in the movie *Without Feathers*, 1976

Page 65, paragraph 2: See, for example, p. 119 in Sigmund Freud, *Civilization and Its Discontents* (W. W. Norton Co., 2005) 75th Anniversary edition with introduction by Louis Menand.

Page 65, paragraph 5: Quoted in a sermon by Dr. George F. Regas, All Saints Church, Pasadena, California

Page 66, paragraph 1: *Shadowlands*, op. cit.

Page 66, paragraph 3: Viorst, p. 344

Page 67, paragraph 1: Leo Tolstoy, *Death of Ivan Ilych and Other Stories* (New York: Signet Classics reissue edition, 1976) paperback, 307 pages

Page 67, paragraph 2: Tolstoy, p. 127

Page 67, paragraph 3: Tolstoy, p. 134

Page 69, paragraph 3: C. S. Lewis, *The Great Divorce* (HarperSanFrancisco 2001) paperback 160 pages; originally published in 1946

Page 71, paragraph 4: "The Blue Green Hills of Earth," Words adapted by Paul Winter from a Ray Bradbury poem; music by Kim Oler (the author's son).

Page 72, paragraph 3: John 14:1-3

Page 73, paragraph 3: "The Great Litany," in *The Book of Common Prayer* according to the use of The Episcopal Church (New York: Oxford University Press, 1979) p. 148: "...from dying suddenly and unprepared, Good Lord, deliver us."

Page 74, paragraph 2: *The Book of Common Prayer*, p. 833, prayer 63, for use "In the Evening."

Page 75, paragraph 3: 1 Corinthians 13:12

Chapter 5: Journey Outward, Journey Inward

Page 81, paragraph 0: Peter DeVries, *The Mackerel Plaza* (Penguin 1986) paperback 272 pages (original hardcover published in Boston by Little Brown in 1958)

Page 82, paragraph 1: Psalm 46:10

Page 83, paragraph 3: Mother Teresa, *A Simple Path* (Ballantine Books, 1995) 240 pages. On page 1 she wrote, "The fruit of silence is PRAYER. The fruit of prayer is FAITH. The fruit of faith is LOVE. The fruit of love is SERVICE. The fruit of service is PEACE." On page 114 she wrote, "Prayer in action is love, and love in action is service."

Page 84, paragraph 2: *The Book of Common Prayer* according to the use of The Episcopal Church (New York: Oxford University Press, 1979) p. 182, Collect for the 19th Sunday after Pentecost.

Chapter 6: Forgiveness
Part I: Deciding to Forgive

Page 86, paragraph 5: Lewis B. Smedes, *Forgive and Forget: Healing the Hurts We Don't Deserve* (HarperCollins Publishers, 1984) 151 pages

Page 87, paragraph 2: Luke 23:34

Page 88, paragraph 1: Matthew 18:22

Page 88, paragraph 2: Matthew 6:9-15

Page 93, paragraph 2: Lt. Cmdr. Bettie J. Davis, "Forgiveness Takes Courage," in the Chapel Pennant column of *Hawaii Navy News Online* (Vol. 4, No. 9, December 10, 1999) available at http://www.hnn.navy.mil/archives/991210/chapel.htm.

Part II: Forgiving Those Who Are Hardest to Forgive

Page 103, paragraph 2: The Amy Biehl Foundation Website is located at http://www.amybiehl.org.

Page 105, paragraph 1: II Corinthians 5:19

Chapter 7: The Spiritual Quest and Psychotherapy

Page 110, paragraph 2: According to information available online, Frederic F. Flach, M.D., K.H.S., is adjunct associate professor of psychiatry at the New York Hospital-Cornell Medical Center and attending psychiatrist at both the Payne Whitney Clinic and St. Vincent's hospital in New York. A practicing psychiatrist for more than thirty years, he is chairman of the board of Directions in Psychiatry, a nationwide education program for psychiatrists, and the author of many books, including *The Secret Strength of Depression* (1974), *A New Marriage, A New Life* (1978), *Resilience* (1988), *Rickie* (1990), *The Seven Habits of Highly Successful Angels* (1998), and *Faith, Healing, and Miracles* (2000). In 1996 he was awarded the Maxine Mason award by the National Alliance for the Mentally Ill (NAMI). He has appeared on numerous radio and television programs across the country, including Today, Good Morning America, CBS This Morning, Good Day New York and Donahue. From an entry in *Contemporary Authors* published by Thomason Gale in 2004:

> Flach is considered one of the nation's experts on the subject of depression. His unique approach to this is to regard the experience of depression itself as a normal phenomenon, becoming a problem when it is too much or lasts too long. With this viewpoint, he sees resilience—the ability to renew oneself after the impact of stress—as the critical factor in health. Such resilience is practically synonymous with the term 'creativity,' and the ability of an individual to engage in renewal depends upon his mental attitudes, his environment, and his physiological systems. In his books for the public, Flach has approached the subject of depression and creativity and, more recently, examined this in the specific concept of marriage, divorce, and remarriage. His view of the human's response to stress not only permits new ways to deal with psychotherapy and research, but also offers a more sensible and effective philosophy for the individual dealing with life changes.

Page 116, paragraph 3: Thomas Merton, *New Seeds of Contemplation* (Boston: Shambhala Publications, 2003), pp. 35-36

Page 117, paragraph 2: Matthew 22:39, Mark 12:31, Luke 10:27

Chapter 8: A Church for Atheists

Page 123, paragraph 2: Kurt Vonnegut, *Slaughterhouse-Five: Or The Children's Crusade, A Duty Dance With Death* (New York: Delacorte Press; 25th Anniversary Edition, 1994) 224 pages

Page 124, paragraph 1: Micah 6:8

Page 125, paragraph 2: Luke 15:11-32

Page 126, paragraph 2: Matthew 27:46; Mark 15:34

Page 127, paragraph 1: C. S. Lewis, *A Grief Observed*, p. 4

Page 128, paragraph 1: William Sloane Coffin told this story with more detail and a little differently to Bill Moyers in an interview available online at http://www.zionsherald.org/May2004_interview.html.

Chapter 9: Children of the Atomic Bomb

Page 132, paragraph 1: Luke 22:19; I Corinthians 11:24-25

Page 132, paragraph 2: Matthew 17:5; Mark 9:7; Luke 9:35

Page 133, paragraph 1: The full statement the mayor delivered August 6, 1995 at the Prayer for Peace Park is available online at http://www.punahou.edu/acad/english/shigemitsu/Hiroshima.html.

Page 134, paragraph 1: Robert Jay Lifton, MD, *Death in Life: Survivors of Hiroshima* (University of North Carolina Press, reprint edition 1991) paperback 594 pages

Page 137, paragraph 2: A biography of Kenzaburo Oe, winner of the 1994 Nobel Prize for Literature, is available at the Nobel Prize Website, http://nobelprize.org/literature/laureates/1994/oe-bio.html.

Page 137, paragraph 2: Kenzaburo Oe, "Denying History," in *The New York Times Magazine*, July 2, 1995, pp. 28-29.

Page 138, paragraph 2: James Kelly, "Thinking about the Unthinkable," *Time Magazine*, Volume 119, No. 13 (March 29, 1982) cover story. See http://www.time.com/time/magazine/0,9263,7601820329,00.html for a picture of the cover, the table of contents—which includes four other related stories—and the text of the articles.

Chapter 10: It Is Toward Evening; the Day Is Far Spent

Page 142, paragraph 2: Luke 24:29

Page 145, paragraph 1: Henri Nouwen and Walter J. Gaffney, *Aging, the Fulfillment of Life*, New York: Doubleday, 1974, page 17.

Chapter 11: The Faith of a Reverent Christian Agnostic

Page 148, paragraph 3: Learned Hand, *The spirit of liberty: Papers and addresses of Learned Hand* (New York: Alfred A. Knopf, 1952), 252 pages. This speech was delivered to a crowd of thousands in New York City's Central Park on "I Am an American Day" on May 21, 1944.

Page 148, paragraph 4: Hand, pp. 190 – 191

Page 150, paragraph 1: Frederick Buechner, *Wishful Thinking: A Theological ABC* (New York: Harper and Row, 1973), p. 32

Page 150, paragraph 2: William Sloane Coffin, *Credo* (Westminster John Knox Press, 2003) page 29

Page 151, paragraph 0: Rabbi Leonard I. Beerman is the founding rabbi, now retired, of Leo Baeck Temple in Brentwood, Los Angeles. He has had a long-time relationship with All Saints Church, which calls him its "Rabbi in Residence." He has participated with George Regas, now Rector Emeritus of All Saints Church, in many peace and justice campaigns and programs.

Page 151, paragraph 2: Matthew 25:35-36, 40

Page 151, paragraph 3: Henry David Thoreau is reported to have said this on his deathbed when asked whether he was prepared for the next world.

Page 151, paragraph 3: Luke 23:43

Page 151, paragraph 4: Isaiah 1:18

Page 152, paragraph 2: Rollo May, *The Courage to Create*, (New York: W. W. Norton & Company, 1994, paperback) p. 21 (as quoted on p. 157 of Coffin, *Credo*)

Page 153, paragraph 0: Coffin, *Credo*, page 9

Page 154, paragraph 2: Blaise Pascal, translated by A. J. Krailsheimer, *Pensees* (Penguin Books, 1995) paperback, 368 pages. The quotation is from *Pensee* #423 on p. 127

Page 155, paragraph 1: E. Stanley Jones, *Mahatma Gandhi: An Interpretation* (New York: Abingdon-Cokesbury, 1948)

Page 156, paragraph 2: Albert Schweitzer, *The Quest of the Historical Jesus: A critical study of its progress from Reimarus to Wrede* (New York: A & C Black, 1936), 410 pages

Page 156, paragraph 3: Schweitzer, p. 403

End Quote

From the well-known Gospel song *Precious Lord, Take My Hand;* words and music by Thomas A. Dorsey (1899-1993), after the tune "Maitland" by George N. Allen (1812-1877).

Printed in the United States
60952LVS00002B/1-180